LIVING BEYOND WORRY AND ANGER

by

Norman Wright

Copyright © 1979 Harvest House Publishers
ISBN 0-89081-194-6
Library of Congress Number 79-83659
Printed in the United States of America

No portion of this material may be reproduced in any form without the written permission of the publisher, except when indicated in the resource for the purpose of presenting the material in a class or meeting and homework assignments.

ADVANCE PREPARATION & OVERVIEW

Session 1: **The Effect of Emotions and Feelings**
1. Have available an overhead projector and the transparency, "Emotions."

Session 2: **Emotional or Cognitive? What are We?**
1. Make sufficient copies of the reproduction master, "Emotions and Feelings."
2. Have available a chalkboard and chalk.

Session 3: **Worry, Concern and Fear**
1. Have available an overhead projector and transparency, "The Effects of Worry."
2. Have available a blank piece of paper and a pencil for each person.

Sessions 4 and 5: **How to Overcome Worry,** The Solution
1. Have available an overhead projector and the transparencies, "The Effects of Worry," "Worry," and "How to Control Worry."
2. Have available a copy of the book, *An Answer to Worry and Anxiety* for each class member. Distribute these at the conclusion of Session 5 and ask them to read the book to reinforce all that you have taught.

Session 6: **Frustration and Anger**
1. Make copies of the reproduction masters, "Frustration Response Form." and "Case Studies on Frustration."

Session 7: **What is Anger?**
1. Have paper, pencils and several boxes of crayons available.

2. Have available the overhead projector and transparency, "Three Words for Anger in the Greek New Testament."

Sessions 8 and 9: **The Causes and Handling of Anger**

1. Have available the overhead projector and transparencies, "Anger," "Anger and the Body," and "The Bible and Anger."

2. Make copies of the reproduction master, "Scripture Application Form."

3. Have available a copy of the book, *"An Answer to Anger and Frustration,"* for each class member. Distribute these at the conclusion of Session 9 and ask them to read the book to reinforce all that you have taught.

Scripture quotations marked RSV are from the REVISED STANDARD VERSION of the Bible, copyrighted 1946, 1952 © 1971, 1973. Used by permission.

Scripture quotations marked TLB are from THE LIVING BIBLE, copyright © 1971, Tyndale House Publishers, Wheaton, Illinois. Used by permission.

Scripture quotations marked AMPLIFIED are from THE AMPLIFIED BIBLE, OLD TESTAMENT, Part I (Genesis-Esther), copyright © 1964 by Zondervan Publishing House; THE AMPLIFIED BIBLE, OLD TESTAMENT, Part II, (Job - Malachi), copyright © 1962 by Zondervan Publishing House; or THE AMPLIFIED NEW TESTAMENT, copyright © The Lockman Foundation 1954, 1958 and are used by permission.

Scripture quotations marked KJV are from the KING JAMES VERSION of the Bible.

All other scripture quotations are from the NEW AMERICAN STANDARD BIBLE, copyright © The Lockman Foundation 1960, 1962, 1963, 1968, 1971, 1972, 1973, 1975 and are used by permission.

Session 1
The Effect Of Emotions and Feelings

TIME: 50-60 minutes
OBJECTIVES:

1. To identify personal beliefs and biblical teaching about feelings and emotions.
2. To clarify one's own awareness and demonstration of emotions.
3. To begin to develop a more positive attitude toward and greater acceptance of feelings and emotions.

ADVANCE PREPARATION:

1. Have available an overhead projector and the transparency, "Emotions."

ACTIVITY: Neighbor-Nudging and Discussion
Time: 5 minutes

Ask each person to turn to the person next to him and for one minute discuss these questions: "What do we mean by the word *emotion?*" "How would you define *emotion?*" After the time is up ask for several responses. In the discussion, share with the class the fact that the word *emotion* is difficult to define. Here are a few definitions that others have developed:

"Emotions are conscious feelings associated with some instinct experienced in the presence of some unusual situation."

"Emotions are mobilized energy."

"An emotional response is similar to a reflex response."

"We detect an emotion in us by 'feeling' it. When we say our feelings impel us to do something, in most cases we mean emotional energy impels us."

"A feeling is an instinctive, unconscious, reflexive physical reaction to a situation. An emotion is the feeling plus the awareness of it."[1]

---
1. Vincent Collins, *Me, Myself & You*, (St. Meinard, In.: Abbey Press, 1976), p. 43.

ACTIVITY: Triads and Discussion
Time: 12-15 minutes

Divide the group into triads or groups of three, choosing people they know the least. Ask them to number off one through three. (When you ask them to start sharing, be sure to begin with person number three, then number one, and then number two.) Tell them that each of them will have two minutes to share with the others in their group. They will be responding to a particular statement which you are going to give them. During the two minutes the others cannot ask any questions but are to listen. At the end of two minutes the others can ask any questions they want to ask and the person who has been sharing must answer. After the first person has finished, then the next person will have two minutes, etc.

The statement they will be responding to is: "This is what you need to know about my emotions and how I handle them in order to understand me as a person."

When everyone has concluded, ask them how they felt during this time and what they learned. Ask what emotions they experienced during this time.

ACTIVITY: Evaluation and Discussion
Time: 25-40 minutes

Show the following emotions on the overhead transparency.

Affectionate	Attracted	Ashamed
Afraid	Belonging	Competitive
Angry	Bored	Defensive
Anxious	Close	Depressed
Fearful	Confused	Disappointed
Frustrated	Inferior	Free
Guilty	Lonely	Sad
Hopeful	Loving	Satisfied
Hurt	Rejected	Shy
Jealous	Respected	Superior
Joyful	Worry	Proud
Trusting		

Ask each person to write his answers to the following questions. After enough time has passed, ask for responses to all of the questions except number two. In the next session we will look further at these questions and draw some conclusions.

1. What emotions and feelings do males exhibit the most? Females?
2. Which of these do you experience and exhibit the most, and which of them does your spouse experience and exhibit the most?
3. Agree or disagree: "Men have different emotions than women."
4. Which of the emotions on the transparency do you feel are wrong?
5. Which of the emotions on the transparency did Jesus experience?

Conclude the session with prayer.

Session 2

Emotional or Cognitive? What Are We?

TIME: 50-60 minutes

OBJECTIVES:

1. To identify personal beliefs and biblical teaching about feelings and emotions.
2. To clarify one's own awareness and demonstration of emotions.
3. To begin to develop a more positive attitude toward and greater acceptance of feelings and emotions.

ADVANCE PREPARATION:

1. Make sufficient copies of the reproduction master, "Emotions and Feelings."
2. Have available a chalkboard and chalk.

ACTIVITY: Lecture
Time: 5-10 minutes

Men do not have different emotions than women. We all have and experience the same emotions, but we may share or display them differently. For example, men generally have a tendency not to allow their emotions or feelings to influence their decisions, whereas women do have a tendency to allow feelings and emotions to be involved in the process of making decisions. One of the reasons why we display emotions differently is our culture conditioning and our home background. Our culture has certain prescribed roles set out for men and women, with prescribed behavior. Fortunately, some of these stereotypes are breaking down.

People allow their emotions to be reflected in the way they communicate. Some communicate on an emotional level, while others operate on a thinking or cognitive level. Persons who communicate primarily on a cognitive level deal mainly with factual data. They like to talk about such topics as sports, the stock market, money, houses, jobs, etc., keeping the subject of conversation out of the emotional area. Usually they become quite uncomfortable if faced with issues that elicit feelings, especially unpleasant feelings such as anger.

Consequently, they avoid talking about subjects that involve love, fear and anger. These persons often have difficulty being warm and supportive of their spouse.

Those who communicate more on the feeling level tire easily of purely factual data and feel a need to share feelings, especially with their spouse. They believe the atmosphere between husband and wife must be as free as possible from such unpleasant feelings as tension, anger, and resentment. They want to talk about these emotional things, resolve conflicts with their spouse, clear the air, and keep things pleasant between them.

Of course no one is completely cognitive or completely emotional.
(Draw this outline on the chalkboard).

```
+--+--+--+--+--+--+--+--+--+--+
Emotional                Cognitive
```

Where are you and where is your spouse on this continuum?

(Ask each person to indicate where he is on this graph, where he thinks his spouse is, and where he thinks his spouse would place him. Then ask the participants to discuss with their spouse for one minute what they have written.)

A person on the left side of the graph, who shares more of their feelings, is not less bright or less intellectual. This person is simply more aware of his feelings and is usually better able to do something about them.

A surprising fact is that the so-called cognitive person (those on the right) is controlled by his feelings just as much as the so-called emotional person, but he does not realize it. For example, the stiff, formal intellectual does have deep feelings, but uses enormous energy to keep them buried so he won't be bothered with them. Unfortunately, they do bother him. Whenever someone (such as an "emotional" wife or child) is around asking him for affection and warmth, he is not only unable to respond, he is angered that his precious equilibrium has been disturbed.[1]

ACTIVITY: Emotions and Feelings
Time: 10-15 minutes

Ask each person to complete the "Emotions and Feelings" form and then to share the results with his or her spouse or in a small group. (Duplicate this form prior to the session.)

LECTURE: Intimacy
Time: 10-20 minutes

Have you ever thought of intimacy as being related to our emotional life? What does intimacy mean to you? Many people consider intimacy as having to do with the physical or sexual relationship. We say, "They are intimate," and mean they had intercourse, but there is more to intimacy than just the physical. It has been suggested that there are three levels of intimacy, and they are arranged in a hierarchy. (Write this on the chalkboard).

```
/  EMOTIONAL    \
/   PHYSICAL     \
/  INTELLECTUAL   \
```

All three of these levels are important, yet some people never seem to attain the emotional level. Everyone has the capacity to attain all of these levels, but for a number of reasons many do not.

INTELLECTUAL INTIMACY is the world of ideas, thoughts, or even roles. People learn to exchange ideas in ways that will protect their inner life rather than expose it. We learn verbal skills that will share the thinking or opinion or belief area of our life, but that doesn't mean that we learn to share how we feel.

PHYSICAL INTIMACY has a tremendous emphasis placed upon it today, and from it couples expect great things. Because of the overemphasis and high expectation attached to it, disappointments have been common. Couples soon learn that physical intimacy does not bring emotional closeness. Often, it does not even bring physical closeness, for that matter. If individuals are looking forward to physical intimacy as an answer to their loneliness and lack of meaning in life, they are soon back at their original state. Often we equate sex with love, but there are significant differences.

EMOTIONAL INTIMACY is the highest level of intimacy. For it to occur four characteristics must be present.

Each person must first be *mutually accessible.* Each has free access to the other person without fear of criticism or restraint. It means a trust and honesty in the relationship that is mutual.

There must also be *naturalness.* Each person is accepted as he is and is not expected to play a role or change to meet the other's requirements. Each can be himself and expose his strengths and weaknesses. Empathy is also a part of the relationship. Each can feel and

---
1. Adapted from D. Ross Campbell, M.D., *How to Really Love Your Child* (Wheaton: SP Publications, 1977), pp. 20-21.

see life as the other. In a natural relationship, feelings are very important and elicit respect from the other person.

Nonpossessiveness is another necessary characteristic. There is no superior or inferior position in the relationship; both are equals. Loving the other person involves allowing him to be independent and not trying to control or possess him. Perhaps this involves seeing the partner who is a Christian as a "joint heir" with Christ. This is also the place where the servanthood model in Ephesians 5 is seen in true demonstration.

The final characteristic involves *process.* Attaining and maintaining emotional intimacy is a process that requires constant attention. Emotional freedom must be worked upon to nurture and develop it so that it continues.

(Note: For additional examples you may want to use the five levels of communication that John Powell talks about in his book *Why Am I Afraid to Tell You Who I Am?* Both his five levels and these four characteristics can be applied to an individual's relationship with God, as found in his prayer life, for example.)

LECTURE: The Bible and Emotions
Time: 10-20 minutes

The scriptures do not tell us directly why we are created with the capacity to feel, to experience emotions. We do know, however, that our emotionality is grounded in the character and nature of God. He has described Himself in the scriptures as having emotions, such as anger *(Deuteronomy 29:20; Joshua 23:16; II Kings 22:13; Ezra 8:22; Job 9:13; Psalms 7:11; 78:12; 106:40; John 3:36; Romans 1:18)*, jealousy *(Deuteronomy 29:20; Psalm 75:58; I Corinthians 10:22)*, and delight *(Isaiah 62:4)*. But God does not experience emotions such as fear, anxiety, and guilt. These, perhaps the most uncomfortable and miserable of human feelings, are apparently experienced by mankind as a result of rebellion against God and would not be experienced otherwise. Could it be that God would not "feel" anger and jealousy except for the rejection of Him by His creation, both angels and people?

The scriptures also record that when God created man He said, "Let Us make man in Our image, according to our likeness," and so "God created man in His own image, in the image of God He created him; male and female He created them" *(Genesis 1:26-27)*. We assume, then, that emotionality reflects an attribute of God in a manner that we are capable of understanding. By experiencing emotions we are better able to know God.

He could have created us without any capacity for feelings. But then, in a very real sense, we would also have been left without the capacity for relationships, with Him or with one another. Those who seem to lack feelings are often referred to as "inhuman." They seem more like machines or hollow shells than people. It is clear then: *We should take delight in our emotional nature.* To eliminate emotions would not only rid us of fear of the dark, sadness over death and anger at inconvenience, but also the satisfaction of a job well done, deep love of one close to us, and hearty laughter at a well-told joke. Without emotions we are hollow people.

Rather than curse and attempt to kill our capacity to feel because we cannot seem to live with our emotions, we should acccept them with joy and exclaim with King David of Israel, "I will give thanks to Thee, for I am fearfully and wonderfully made" *(Psalm 139:14)*.

The Bible gives many examples of men who experienced deep emotions. (Share the following scriptures with the class, using the Amplified version: *Genesis 4:4-5; 29:20; Habakkuk 3:16; Romans 12:15; II Corinthians 6:10; Ephesians 4:26; II Timothy 1:7).*

Emotions are a mixed blessing. They are responsible for man's finest and greatest achievements. They are also responsible for some of the greatest tragedies in our world. Our emotions play a large part in making our lives meaningful or miserable.

C. B. Eavey, in his book *Principles of Mental Health for Christian Living,* suggested: "Nothing in us so defiles and destroys the beauty and the glory of living as do emotions; nothing so elevates, purifies, enriches, and strengthens life as does emotion. Through our emotions we can have the worst or the best, we can descend to the lowest depths or we can rise to the highest heights. Every normal human being has a longing for the overflowing of natural emotion. Without capacity to experience emotions suitable to situations we meet, we would not be normal. Emotions of the right kind, expressed in the proper way, make life beautiful, full, and rich, rob it of monotony, and contribute much to both the enjoyment and the effectiveness of living."[2]

Our emotions are a gift from God for we were created as emotional beings. Because of the fall, man's emotional life often becomes distorted. But our emotion as such should never be despised, expelled, ignored, or even neglected. "If we try to drive away any one of them," adds Eavey, "we simply intensify its activity. When we let them go without guidance and control, they cause confusion and riot in our lives. If we try to suppress them, they produce destruction in our personalities."

As we consider our emotions we may find that we are a person who experiences some of them too deeply and intensely (such as worry, anger, or depression). On the other hand, we may not be in touch with some of them sufficiently or we may deny them and never share either the positive or the negative ones. A speaker once said, "When Jesus went to the cross for us, He also went to the cross for our emotional life."

ACTIVITY: Prayer
Time: 5-10 minutes

Conclude the session by asking couples to pray together thanking God for their emotions and feelings. Have them ask God to help them either control some of their intense feelings and expressions, if that is a concern in their life, or free them to experience and express themselves more.

Session 3

Worry, Concern And Fear

TIME: 60 minutes
OBJECTIVES:

1. To clarify the meaning of fear, worry, and anxiety.
2. To identify the effects of worry, the biblical teaching and insights about worry.
3. To list biblical patterns of overcoming worry.

ADVANCE PREPARATION:

1. Have available an overhead projector and the transparency, "The Effects of Worry."
2. Have available a blank piece of paper and a pencil for each person.

ACTIVITY: Introductory Lecture
Time: 5-10 minutes

Death was walking toward the city, and a man stopped Death and asked, "What are you going to do?" Death said, "I'm going to kill 10,000 people." The man said, "That's horrible." Death said, "That's the way it is. That's what I do." So the day passed. The man met Death coming back, and he said, "You said you were going to kill 10,000 people, and there were 70,000 killed!" Death said, "I only killed 10,000. Worry and fear killed the others."

What is the difference between fear, concern and worry? (Ask the class to spend one minute discussing this question with the person sitting next to them. Ask for several responses.)

Write the following statement on the board. "The Bible teaches that anxiety is a part of our lives and we should expect it to occur." Ask the class to indicate by raising their

---
2. C.B. Eavey, *Principles of Mental Health for Christian Living*, (Chicago, Ill: Moody Press, 1956), p. 164.

hands how many agree with the statement and how many disagree. Then ask the class to share their responses with two others for several minutes.

ACTIVITY: Lecture
Time: 25-35 minutes

FEAR

Often we use the words "fear," "worry," and "anxiety" interchangeably, but there are distinct differences between the three. It is important that we be aware of the distinction. *Fear* is an emotional response which is consciously recognized and is usually stimulated by a real problem. We know what the problem is and we feel afraid because of it. If you are driving down the highway and somebody swerves into your lane and is coming at you head-on, it is normal for you to be afraid. If not, you will be in real trouble! If you walk into a yard without believing the sign that says "Beware of Dog" and suddenly a 185-pound dog comes leaping at you, you will probably have a fear response.

Fear is the legitimate protective response. We need to be able to experience fear, because it protects us from harm.

Years ago an experiment was conducted with firemen. Most firemen have a healthy fear response toward fire. But under hypnosis psychologists took away that fear response and then, under controlled conditions, allowed the firemen to fight a fire. Each man who had been hypnotized was assigned to another man who had not gone through the experiment. The firemen who had undergone hypnosis went into deadly situations that they would ordinarily avoid. Their unhypnotized partners had to restrain them from taking unnecessary risks. Obviously, the fear response that they ordinarily had was very important. After the experiment the psychologists put them back under hypnosis and restored the fear response so they were capable of fulfilling their jobs in safety.

ANXIETY

Another word that is used extensively is *anxiety*. Close your eyes right now and try to imagine what it feels like to experience anxiety. How would you describe it? (Ask for several responses). If you said anxiety was a feeling of dread, you were right. It is a feeling of apprehension or uneasiness which produces a sense of approaching danger which doesn't always stem from a reasonable cause. Perhaps you have been in a situation where you felt on edge or shaky. You felt bothered and tense but could not put your finger on any reason for your feelings. That is anxiety. Some people experience what we call "anxiety states." The hands shake, the heart pounds, perspiration pours out. They feel that something is desperately wrong, but don't know what it is. This is the extreme form of anxiety.

WORRY

Worry is a cousin to fear and anxiety. Worry is a state of fearfulness that can be tied into a problem situation, either imagined or real. There is no sharp line of separation between worry and anxiety. The words are often used interchangeably, but the word "worry" actually means to fret or to be overly concerned.

Another definition of worry can give us an important insight. The word means a mind that has been divided; thus the one who worries has a divided mind. John Haggai's book *How to Win Over Worry* contains this description of worry: "Worry divides the feelings; therefore, convictions are shallow and changeable. Worry divides the faculty of perception; therefore, observation is faulty and even false. Worry divides the faculty of judging; therefore, attitudes and decisions are often unjust."[1]

Another definition of worry is that a worried person has activated the powers of his imagination to blow a real or perceived problem out of proportion. You probably know what it's like to try to sleep at night when you have something on your mind. You lie there trying to get to sleep, but soon you start mulling over the situation or problem. You go through it once, then again, and then another time. It is interesting that the second time you start thinking it through, you amplify and add to some of the events. And the fifth time you run

---

1. John Edmund Haggai, *How to Win Over Worry*, (Grand Rapids, Mich.: Zondervan, 1959), p. 17.

through it, it's really blown out of proportion. Some people find themselves lying in bed almost rigid, tight as a drum!

Worry is identified by the question, "What if . . .?" What if this happened, what if that happened, what if, what if, what if!"

CONCERN

There is a difference between worry and concern. Concern involves being bothered or troubled about a specific situation or condition. It could be that you are wondering, "What is going to happen when my daughter goes to high school next year?" "Is it going to be a good school?" or, "Is it going to be a poor school?" "How is she going to deal with some of the new concepts that she is going to run into?" This is what we would call concern. Worry comes when you spend time each day going over and over it in your mind. "What if she gets in with the wrong crowd?" "What if there are drugs there?" "What if she gets some bad teachers?" "What if her teachers don't like her because she is a Christian?" You can expand the problem out of perspective and that is what we call worry.

Concern, on the other hand, is justified. If you are concerned about your daughter, you could go to the high school, meet the teachers, and ask about the philosophy, the curriculum, or the extra-curricular activities. Concern leads to concrete action.

At this point in your presentation take a few minutes and ask each member in the class to write down the answers to the following questions without discussing them with anyone else. (Provide paper and pencils).

1. What did you worry about this past week?
2. How much time did you spend in worry? Please be specific.
3. What did your worry accomplish?

THE EFFECTS OF WORRY

Have you ever stopped to think what worry does for you? What does it accomplish? You may be like the person who said, "I've worried for twenty years. I'm so good at it, I'm a professional worrier." But where does it get you? (Use the overhead transparency for highlighting the main points).

Scripture has this to say about the effects of worry and fear: "I heard and my [whole inner self] trembled, my lips quivered at the sound. Rottenness enters into my bones and under me—down to my feet . . ." *(Habakkuk 3:16, Amplified)*. This writer experienced that intense fear that almost immobilizes a person. *Proverbs 12:25* says, "Anxiety in a man's heart weighs it down" *(Amplified)*. That is so graphic! If you're struggling under a load of worry or depression, you actually feel like there is a heavy weight on your body, and you don't function as you ordinarily would.

Another passage in Proverbs gives the opposite to the life of worry: "A tranquil mind gives life to the flesh" *(Proverbs 14:30, RSV)*.

What happens if you have a mind that is constantly in gear for worrying? The worry can eventually have an effect upon your body—an ulcer, for example, where part of the body is actually destroyed or eaten away. *Proverbs 15:15* says, "All the days of the desponding afflicted are made evil [by anxious thoughts and forebodings]" *(Amplified)*. Dr. Vernon Grounds, President of the Conservative Baptist Seminary in Denver, illustrates this point: "The fear-ridden person may be so uptight that he becomes either rigid or hyperactive, incapable of seeing things realistically because anxiety is distorting his perspective. He may, because of anxiety, be incapable of acting or reacting efficiently."[2]

In a familiar passage about anxiety, *Matthew 25:24-25* states, "Then he which had received the one talent came and said, Lord, I knew thee, that thou art an hard man, reaping where thou hast not sown and gathering where thou hast not strewn, and I was afraid and went and hid thy talent in the earth" *(KJV)*. In this parable of the talent Jesus is pointing out that anxiety or fear squelches responsibility. It inhibits productive activity, stifles initiative, and drains off courage. We could actually miss out on some of the great opportunities of life because of intense fear. It simply comes down to the point that we have to be willing to run the risk of reaching out.

---

2. From "The Bible and Anxiety," by Dr. Vernon Grounds, *Christian Herald*, December 1974, page 27.

In interpersonal relationships we find that a person who is not willing to run the risk of being hurt cannot be involved in a love relationship with another individual. For example, there are many students who have said, "I was really hurt last year by this girl, and I just don't know if I want to attempt it again. I sure would like to be in love with somebody and get married." They have to overcome that worry—they must be willing to run the risk of opening their life to the extent that they could be hurt.

Most people are familiar with the story of Mary and Martha. "Now it came to pass, as they went, that he entered into a certain village: and a certain woman named Martha received him into her house. And she had a sister called Mary, which also sat at Jesus' feet and heard his word. But Martha was cumbered about with much serving, and came to him, and said, Lord, dost thou not care that my sister hath left me to serve alone? Bid her therefore that she help me" *(Luke 10:38-40, KJV)*. The excessive activity, the busyness of a Martha or her male counterpart, may be motivated by anxiety. The tense and troubled person is apt to be almost frantically active. His inability to relax prevents him from enjoying even God's greatest blessings.

Some anxious people become overinvolved. Others say to them, "I don't see how you can do it—running a home, you're here at five different meetings . . ." We reinforce them in their busyness, not thinking that their busyness may be the result of some fear or anxiety in their life.

Another passage which shows the result of worry is *Luke 8:14:* "And that which fell among thorns are they, which, when they have heard, go forth, and are choked with cares (or anxieties) and riches and pleasures of this life, and bring no fruit to perfection" *(KJV)*. Worry and anxiety actually have a tendency to stifle our spiritual growth.

There is another way of looking at the effect of worry or anxiety. When you worry about a particular problem, the problem is magnified. Worry prevents you from thinking logically about the subject. The reasons for this is simple. When you worry, you may experience actual bodily changes as certain glands overrespond to your mental state. Your thinking ability is lessened because of the physiological changes occurring within you.

Perhaps you have experienced this sort of physiological change in connection with anger. A friend rubs you the wrong way, and you flare up at him. Later you confess, "When I get angry like that, I just don't think straight. I can't think of the right thing to say. I just shout."

We humans are so constructed that when we experience an intense emotion we cannot think as clearly as usual. Later, when we're out of the situation and the emotions have subsided, we can see the facts in clearer perspective.

Worry can paralyze us and prevent us from doing things constructively. The most capable person may become so tied up in worry that he or she becomes less and less effective. Problems call for decisions and action, but when you worry you cannot decide and therefore you do not act. Worry makes you indecisive. The most decisive and clear-thinking people can immobilize themselves by going over and over the problem; in the end they still cannot decide, and they leave the decision to another.

ACTIVITY: Group Discussion
Time: 20 minutes

Ask the class members to work in groups of four to six to discuss these questions: What are Christians most likely to worry about? What do your family members worry about the most? What can you do to help them overcome the worry? After they have discussed these questions for ten minutes ask them to spend five minutes sharing their answers to the three questions asked earlier. Then have several members share with the class their answers to the question of what Christians worry about most and what family members can do to help other family members overcome their worry.

Conclude with prayer.

Session 4 and 5
How to Overcome Worry, The Solution

TIME: Approximately 2 hours
OBJECTIVES:
1. To identify biblical teaching and insights about worry.
2. To develop biblical patterns of overcoming worry.

ADVANCE PREPARATION:
1. Have available an overhead projector and the transparencies, "The Effects of Worry," "Worry," and "How to Control Worry."
2. Have available a copy of the book, *"An Answer to Worry and Anxiety"* for each class member. Distribute at the conclusion of Session 5 and ask them to read the book to reinforce all that you have taught.

Note: This section of material is designed for two sessions. You will need to decide where to conclude Session 4 based upon how much you can cover.

ACTIVITY: Lecture
Time: 30-40 minutes

Wayne Dyer, the well-known author and lecturer, has stated: "You could take the ten best worriers in the entire world. Put them in the same room for the rest of their lives and allow them to worry and worry only. And you know what would happen? Absolutely nothing!"[1]

There is an old Moorish proverb that states: "He who is afraid of a thing gives it power over him."

WORRY—THE SELF-FULFILLING PROPHECY

Worry and fear can become self-fulfilling prophecies. Job 3:25-26 says, "For the thing which I greatly fear is come upon me, and that which I was afraid of is come upon me" *(KJV)*. You can bring about the very thing that you fear the most. If you worry about having an accident when you drive, you're the last person most of us would want to drive with. Statistically, you are highly likely to cause an accident. Your mind is so occupied with the thought of an accident that you help to bring it about.

A salesman new to the job may worry about the impression he will make on his customers. "What if I forget part of my sales pitch? What if they ask a question I can't answer? What if they have complaints about the product?" He worries so much that all his thinking is going in that direction. When he does get in to see a customer, he does indeed make mistakes. And then he'll say to himself, "I knew this was going to happen! My worry was legitimate—I should have worried even more!"

One of the most common worries concerns rejection. A person will wonder, "What are other people going to think of me? Will they like me or not? I wonder what will happen when I walk into that new group? What if they don't speak to me? What if I speak to a new person and he says just a couple of words and then turns away?" People spend their time worrying, and then when they go into a group, they don't speak or act naturally. Their behavior gives people the feeling that they are different or strange.

WORRY AND YOUR IMAGINATION

Why do you worry? Is it because of your circumstances? If you moved to a better neighborhood or changed jobs, would you stop worrying? No, you would not. You worry because you have an imagination, not because of your circumstances. Imagination is a beautiful gift from God, but like every other gift it can be abused. (Use the overhead transparency, "The Effects of Worry," for the two quotes). Vincent Collins said, "Imagination is to the emotions what illustrations are to a text, what music is to a ballad. It is the ability to form mental pictures, to visualize irritating or fearful situations in concrete form."[1]

---

1. Vincent Collins, *Me, Myself and You,* (St. Meinard, In.: Abbey Press, 1974), used by permission.

Alexander White has wonderfully described this greatest of all gifts which God has given us. He says of the imagination, "It makes us full of eyes, without and within. The imagination is far stronger than any other power which we possess, and psychologists tell us that on occasion when the will and the imagination are in conflict, the imagination wins. How important, therefore, that we should vow, by the Saviour's help, never to throw the wrong kind of pictures on the screen in our minds, for the imagination literally has the power of making the things that we picture very real and effective."[2]

Our imagination can do strange things to us. A classic illustration of its power concerns a man who was driving in the country and had a flat tire. He found that he had a spare tire but no jack. He saw a farmhouse about a mile down the road, so he figured, "I'll just walk down there and borrow a jack." As he walked down the road he got to thinking, "I hope it's a friendly farmer, and I hope he doesn't have any of those big dogs around that I've seen before. You know, he could be a really unfriendly type. He might even try to run me off, he might be rude to me, he might sic his dogs on me, he might be downright nasty about it."

And so the motorist walked along, using his imagination in this negative way. He reached the farmhouse and knocked at the door. The farmer came to the door and graciously said, "Yes, can I help you?" And the man said, "You can keep your old jack! I didn't want it in the first place!" That is an illustration of the power of our imagination.

What happens when your teen daughter is late coming home from a date? She is ten minutes late and you wonder what she and her date are up to, where they are, why they didn't call, what if . . . What if . . . ? The main question of worry. It can bring all types of problems to mind.

When your daughter is late, what can you do to avoid wasting your energy in useless worry? You can commit her—and your worries—to God in prayer. If you know where she and her date were supposed to be, you can phone and find out if they are there.

Finally, when they do come home, learn to avoid overreacting with "Where in the world have you been?" and a long lecture about thoughtlessness and irresponsibility. You may discover that they had a flat tire and there was no phone nearby. Try this approach: "It was getting late, and I was really getting concerned. What happened?" That will help the young people share what happened without getting defensive; and you are in better control of yourself. Then you can say, "Look, the next time this happens, what do you think we could do so that I would be notified? I was really getting afraid because you were an hour late." That is a much healthier way of presenting your fear to another person.

In *Genesis 6:5* we find the very first time that the word "imagination" is used in the Scripture. It is interesting to note how it is presented. "The Lord saw that the wickedness of man was great in the earth, and that every imagination and intention of all human thinking was only evil continually" *(Amplified)*. The first time imagination is mentioned in the Scriptures, we learn that it is evil. Our imagination is creating a problem.

Genesis 8:21 says, "I will never again curse the ground because of man, for the imagination . . . of man's heart is evil and wicked from his youth" *(Amplified)*. *Isaiah 26:3* states, "Thou wilt keep him in perfect peace whose mind (or imagination) is stayed on thee" *(KJV)*. The inner peace and stability that we're looking for will come when we have our thought life truly focused on and directed toward God.

A man once said, "It is impossible to live in the present without also living in the past and the future. By way of memory I re-image my past, and by way of anticipatory imagination, I pre-image my future."

It is impossible for us to live only in the here and now, because the past affects us and we are looking forward to the future. But the effects of the past and the future may be positive or negative. For example, if you keep looking back to the past with regret—"What if I hadn't said that . . . I wish I hadn't done that. . ."—that can keep you tied down in the present. Or you can create a problem with the

---

2. Alexander White: as quoted by Hannah Hurnard in *Winged Life*. Used by permission from Artype Services, Portland Oregon.

future by asking the question, "What if . . .?" and by imagining all the difficult things that might happen.

STEPS TO OVERCOMING WORRY

In order to overcome worry, you need to start by identifying what you worry about. Earl Nightengale once shared a study on what people worry about, and found that *40 percent of our worries are about things that never happen.* How many things have you worried about that never happened? Ask for some examples from the group. (Use the overhead transparency, "Worry.")

The researcher found that *30 percent of people's worries concern things that are in the past,* which can't be changed by worry. A person will think, "Oh, good grief, why did I ever do that? Why did I ever say that? If only I had come from the right sort of home, these things wouldn't have happened to me." He spends time going over and over some experience of the past and worrying about its lasting effects on his life.

Twelve percent of our worries are needless concerns about our health. You get up in the morning, feeling not quite up to par, and you wonder if you're coming down with something. "I ran into that man with that strange cough yesterday—I wonder if I picked it up." Though we often need to have more positive concern about caring properly for our bodies, plain worry doesn't accomplish anything, and can be detrimental.

Ten percent of our worries the researcher designated as *petty, miscellaneous worries*—not worth worrying about. That leaves a total of *8 percent for real, legitimate concerns.*

If you're really serious about overcoming worry, this is the time and the place for you to do some work.

ACTIVITY: Evaluation and Planning
Time: 15 minutes

Ask the class to take a piece of paper and a pencil. Take your time as you go through these next steps in class, asking each person to write down six to eight worries from the past two months.

After several minutes ask them to go back through the list and see how many of their worries are things that may never happen; how many concern the past, which they cannot change; how many may be needless worries about their health; how many are petty; and how many are cause for real concern.

Then ask them to write down how much time they spent worrying in the last week. This may not be easy to pin down, but they should try. "How many minutes—or hours—did you spend worrying?"

Ask them to select one of their worries which they have determined is a genuine cause of concern. Then, instead of worrying about it, make a plan for dealing with it. Write out the plan, step by step, on the piece of paper.

ACTIVITY: Lecture
Time: 20-35 minutes

Earl Lee, in his book *Recycled for Living,* says, "Tension is normal and natural in life. Without tension, we could not exist any more than a violin string can be played without being stretched across the bridge. This creative tension is not the same thing as destructive worry. Worry is like racing an automobile engine while it is in neutral. The gas, the noise, and the smog do not get us anywhere. But legitimate concern is putting the car into low gear on your way to moving ahead. You tell yourself you are going to use the power God has given you to do something about the situation which should cause you to fret."[3]

Solving a problem means putting our concern and energy into low gear, not going from low gear to high, but using a gradual, building process. Look over the plan you made for dealing with your worry. Does it start in low gear? Does it provide for gradual shifting into second and then into high? Don't try to solve a problem all in one great leap; make it a process.

You can see an illustration of a step-by-step process in the way a non-swimmer who is afraid of the water learns to swim. Let's call him Bill. If you were to ask Bill, "Wouldn't you like to learn to swim," he would probably reply, "No, I wouldn't."

Two things are going on in Bill's mind. First, he's trying to see himself swimming the

---
3. Earl Lee, *Recycled for Living,* (Glendale, Ca.: Regal Books, 1973).

length of the pool several times, and he just can't believe that he'll ever be able to do that.

Second, he's seeing himself plunging into the water in the deep end, thrashing around, gulping water, panicking, and drowning.

The way for Bill to face his fear of the water—the way to control fear and worry in general—is to do it gradually.

The conquest of Bill's fear begins in his mind. He should sit in a chair and imagine going up to the edge of the pool; he looks at the water and notices how calm it is; he observes that there's a lifeguard at hand. Then he pictures himself sitting on the edge of the pool with his feet in the water. That's not too scary. When he's comfortable with that thought, he sees himself wading around in the shallow end.

Eventually Bill will turn thought into action and will actually step further into the shallow end of the pool. Day after day he will do only as much as he can do comfortably—but each day he will try to do a little more, to go a little deeper. The water will be up to his knees, then his waist, then his chest. Eventually he'll get someone to help him learn to float, and then to swim.

Have you ever bought something and later discovered that it was defective? Did you worry about how the clerk would act when you returned it? That's a common worry experience. Here, too, the step-by-step procedure is helpful. Begin by writing down the basic facts—when you bought the item, what's wrong with it, why you think you're entitled to a refund. Now practice saying all this out loud. Get in front of a mirror and practice it. Practice on family members. Keep this up until you feel relaxed and at ease. Then you can face the clerk and you'll be more prepared than he is; you'll probably have no trouble at all stating your case.

Scripture provides many helpful principles to follow in overcoming worry. Let's take a look at some of them. (Use the overhead transparency, "Worry," throughout this section where it is applicable).

STOP WORRYING

The Bible just comes right out and says it: "Don't worry!" The Apostle Paul said it very clearly in *Philippians 4:6-9:*

> Do not fret or have any anxiety about anything, but in every circumstance and in everything by *prayer* and petition [definite requests] with thanksgiving continue to make your wants known to God. And God's *peace* [be yours . . . that peace] which transcends all understanding, shall garrison and mount guard over your hearts and minds in Christ Jesus. For the rest, brethren, whatever is true, whatever is worthy of reverence and is honorable and seemly, whatever is just, whatever is pure, whatever is lovely and lovable, whatever is kind and winsome and gracious, if there is any virtue and excellence, if there is anything worthy of praise, *think on* and weigh and take account of these things—fix your minds on them. *Practice* what you have learned and received and heard and seen in me, and model your way of living on it, and the God of peace—of untroubled, undisturbed well-being—will be with you *(Amplified).*

Paul says not to worry. The sense is "Stop worrying." Not, "If you feel like stopping, stop," but, *"Stop it!"* Not, "If your circumstances are comfortable," but *"In every circumstance!"* No matter what's happening to you, make your wants known to God, and don't worry. God promises you His peace if you will do that. It doesn't say that your circumstances will change, but that His peace will guard your heart.

Verse eight tells you what to think about—"Whatever is true, pure, lovely," and so on. Fill your heart and mind with good things and you won't have so much room for worry.

Don't stop at verse eight, though. Verse nine is important: it tells us to *practice* what we have learned. Many people make an effort to do as the Bible says, but they try it just once and then say, "It doesn't work." You've got to do it over and over again—you've got to *practice* living God's way.

One way to practice thinking God's way is to take a 3 x 5 card and on one side write the word "STOP" in big letters. On the other side of the card write out Philippians 4:6-9. Keep the card available in your pocket or in your purse. Whenever you begin to worry, pull out the card. If you are at home or in a place where no one else is around, hold the card in front of you and say the word "STOP" out loud. Then turn it over and read the Scripture out loud. If you are in the presence of others, read it to yourself so you don't give them the impression that you are strange.

The action of taking out that card and reading it will stop your worrying and will focus your mind on the positive input from the Scripture. This breaks the cycle of worry. The longer you let worry go on, the more difficult it is to stop; you must do something tangible to break the pattern.

Eventually you can get to the point where you don't need the card any more—you just remind yourself to "STOP." Then you start going over the Scripture, which you have memorized by now. As you put this Scripture into practice, you develop stability in your life and you begin to see that the Word of God is true and is effective. It takes consistent effort and practice to achieve results. Some people keep several cards around the house so that they have them available at any time.

LET LOOSE OF YOUR CARES

Another passage of Scripture that relates to worry is I Peter 5:7: "Casting all your anxiety upon Him because He cares for you."

Peter tells us what we're to do and why we're to do it. The word "cast" means to give up. A French version translates it *"unload your cares onto God."* Cast means "having deposited with;" it refers to a direct, once-and-for-all committal to God of all that would give a person concern.

A college student was having some trouble with worry; he was fretting over several genuine problems, but his worry was not constructive. In an effort to remind himself that God would help him, he cut out some letters and stuck them up on his bulletin board. They read, "Let God." It was a comfort, but he still kept worrying. Then one day a breeze blew in and made the "d" fall down. When the student looked at his message, it read, "Let Go." He got the point.

All our worries are to be cast onto the Lord; and the reason we can cast these cares on God with confidence is that He cares for us.

GOD KNOWS OUR LIMITS

God knows how much we can take. Isaiah 42:3 says: A bruised reed He will not break, and a dimly burning wick He will not extinguish."

God knows how much we can bear; He knows the limit that each of us has, and as we approach that limit He is there so that we do not move past it and break under the strain.

FRET NOT, BUT INSTEAD . . .

Psalm 37 has been called a psalm for the answer to worry. It begins by saying:

Fret not yourself because of evildoers, neither be envious against those who work unrighteousness . . . Trust (lean on, rely on and be confident) in the Lord, and do good . . . Delight yourself also in the Lord, and He will give you the desires and secret petitions of your heart. Commit your way to the Lord—roll and repose [each care of] your road on Him; trust (lean on, rely on and be confident) also in Him, and He will bring it to pass . . . Be still and rest in the Lord . . . *(vv. 1, 3-5, 7, Amplified).*

"Fret" is an interesting term—it means to eat away, to gnaw, to worry, agitate, or wear away. When you are worrying, you are eating away at yourself. Worry can have an effect on your body, as we discussed earlier.

Psalm 37 gives four basic principles to counteract worry: *Trust* in the Lord, *delight* in the Lord, *commit* your way to the Lord, *rest* in the Lord.

Trusting and committing involve completely letting go, flinging yourself upon God, dislodging the burden onto God, or releasing it to Him. It means that you can go to the Lord and say, "Lord, I'm concerned about this, but I'm going to give it to you. When I finish praying I expect that this is not going to be on my mind anymore. I can rest in the confidence that you are working even though I don't know the outcome. It might come out differently than I anticipate, but it's not something that I have to carry around any more."

At this point, ask for a volunteer to come forward. Ask the person if they trust you. If they say yes, ask them if they trust you enough if you were to ask them to turn around and fall backwards into your arms. Ask the person to turn around and to do this when you say "fall." (Be sure to catch the person!) After he has done this share with the class that this is exactly what the words trust and commit mean—letting go and flinging yourself onto others.

Delighting also means that you enjoy the Lord for who He is—not just for what He can do for you. Enjoying God's presence is a trait most of us need to cultivate. Here's a way you might work on it: begin by praying about the problem that's troubling you, but spend only about 10 percent of your prayer time on the problem. Use the remaining 90 percent for praising and worshipping the Lord for Himself. This will take your mind off your problem and focus it on the Lord.

Rest means to cease, to be silent, to submit in silence to what He ordains. Many people say, "I'd really like to put that into practice, but when I sit down or lie down at night I'm tense. I don't relax." Along with reading the Scripture and committing this to the Lord, there are some exercises you can do to promote relaxation.

When you sit down or lie down, purposely tense up some of the muscles in your body—maybe in your arms or legs. Let them tense up for several seconds, until you feel that you are straining. Then release the muscles and notice the surge of relaxation that comes into them. As you focus on this good feeling you will be lessening your overall tension.

Here's another exercise: Sit in a comfortable chair. Begin with your hands; visualize them as having no strength. Let them flop around and be very free. Then visualize your arms as being very loose and free, as though there were no weight on them at all. Follow this procedure until you have relaxed all the parts of your body. After ten or fifteen minutes, your problem may be, "How do I get motivated to get up and get back to work?" That sort of "problem" is very healthy for a person who needs to learn to relax!

As you learn to relax your body, your mind will learn to relax. Instead of feeling the tension of the body, you'll be able to concentrate on visualizing the presence of the Lord. You'll be focusing on Him rather than on your worries. (Use transparency, "How to Control Worry.")

FREEDOM FROM WORRY DOES NOT DEPEND ON CIRCUMSTANCES

Many people think that it would take a change of circumstances to give them peace of mind. But that is not what the Word of God teaches! God does not promise His children ideal circumstances; He doesn't say that you will never have trials or problems or difficulties. Instead, He says through His word that *in spite of* the pain, the torment and the turmoil, you can have inner stability. Proverbs 15:15 says: "All the days of the desponding afflicted are made evil [by anxious thoughts and foreboding], but he who has a glad heart has a continual feast [regardless of circumstances]" *(Amplified)*.

No matter what you are going through, you can have peace and stability in your life. It takes an act of the will to continually turn your mind to God and away from your problems; it takes discipline, but the result is peace.

ACTIVITY: Bible Study
Time: 10 minutes

PRAISE THE LORD *FIRST*

Ask the class in groups of three to read II Chronicles 20. Ask them to discover the principles of praise in this passage which we can follow. Following a brief discussion, summarize with the lecture material.

ACTIVITY: Lecture
Time: 20-35 minutes

The story of Jehoshaphat, in II Chronicles 20, (Amplified) provides an interesting illustration of the principle of praising the Lord. "After this the Moabites, the Ammonites, and with them Meunites, came against Jehoshaphat to battle. It was told Jehoshaphat, a great multitude has come against you" *(vv. 1, 2)*.

Jehoshaphat had a problem: several other countries were sending armies to fight him.

"Then Jehoshaphat feared" *(v. 3)* He heard the news, and immediately he was afraid. That was a legitimate fear. There are times when we ought to be fearful.

But what did Jehoshaphat do with his fear? He "set himself to seek the Lord" *(v. 3)*. He didn't waste time in fruitless worry; he brought his problem to the Lord. He gathered the people of Judah together, and then prayed to the Lord.

Jehoshaphat prayed, "O our God, will You not exercise judgment upon them? For we have no might to stand against this great company that is coming against us" *(v. 12)*. In other words, "Lord, we don't have what it takes to deal with the problem." Then he said, in effect, "We don't know what to do, but, Lord, our eyes are upon You."

When you're dealing with a problem, admit your inadequacy to deal with it. "I don't know what to do, but, Lord, my eyes are upon You and I'm looking to You for help."

After Jehoshaphat prayed, the Holy Spirit moved a man named Jahaziel to say, "Hearken, all Judah, you inhabitants of Jerusalem and you King Jehoshaphat, the Lord says this to you: Be not afraid or dismayed at this great multitude; for the battle is not yours but God's" *(v. 15)*.

The problems that you and I are dealing with are not really ours—they are God's, and He is involved. We need to recognize this and take hold of it in our thinking. We can pray something like this: "Lord, Your Word says the battle is not mine but Yours. I acknowledge that fact right now. I recognize that this problem is Yours. I praise You for Your power to solve it. I lay down my claim to the problem; I leave it in Your hands." You may have to pray that way many times before your emotions are convinced—but keep at it. God will honor your effort.

The next thing that happened is most interesting: three different groups of people stood up to praise the God of Israel "with a very loud voice" *(v. 19)*. They were facing a battle, and they started praising the Lord.

"When he had consulted with the people, he appointed singers to sing to the Lord and praise Him in their holy garments, as they went out before the army, saying, 'Give thanks to the Lord, for His mercy and loving kindness endure forever!' And when they began to sing and to praise, the Lord set ambushments against the men . . . who had come against Judah" *(vv. 21-22)*. ***When*** they began to sing and to praise, ***then*** the Lord moved. You could properly insert that word ***then***: "***Then*** the Lord did this."

Many people say, "Lord, take care of the problem, then I will sing to you and praise you." Praising God first is a difficult principle to follow; often we just don't feel like praising Him, and we will struggle against the idea that we should do it. We might have to say to Him, "Lord, I know Your Word says to praise You. I'd like to do it, but it's hard. However, I'm just going to go ahead and try it on faith; I'm going to thank You in advance, even though I don't know how it's going to come out."

To the degree that we believe and trust God, to that degree will we be successful. Sometimes we do not like to hear a statement like this because we are in the depths of a struggle and we find it difficult to grasp this concept. Yet if we can come to the place where we employ the principles of trusting and praising God, we find that they work.

LEARN TO BE CONTENT— IT CAN HAPPEN!

The Apostle Paul, who was intimately acquainted with problems and suffering, wrote,

> Not that I am implying that I was in any personal want, for I have learned how to be content in whatever state I am. I know how to be abased, and live humbly in straitened circumstances and I know also how to enjoy plenty and live in abundance. I have learned in any and all circumstances, the secret of facing every situation, whether well-fed or going hungry, having a sufficiency and to spare or going without and being in want *(Philippians 4:11-12, Amplified)*.

He said he had *learned* how to be content. It was a process. It didn't happen overnight. He had to learn, and I believe he did it through his relationship with Jesus Christ. If Paul learned that lesson—if he could sing hymns in the Philippian jail—we, too, can learn to be content.

(Take a blank sheet of paper and make a large dot in the middle. Hold it up in front of the class and ask them to tell you what they see. Most of them will say that they see the dot. You could respond with something like "You see a large dot. Why don't you see the 98 percent of the paper that is totally blank? Because it's human nature to focus on the problem!")

Maybe your problems amount to 2 percent of your life. When you focus exclusively on problems, you are ignoring the 98 percent that is going well. Try asking yourself what you can learn from the 98 percent that would help solve the problem in the 2 percent. Learn to focus on the positive things. (Ask for specific examples from the group as to ways they have learned to be content in the midst of difficulty.)

LEARN TO CONTROL YOUR THOUGHTS

Focusing on the positive, learning to defeat worry—all these involve your thought life. (Use the transparency, "How to Control Worry.") Scripture teaches that it is possible to control our own thoughts. It takes the work of the Holy Spirit combined with our efforts to do it. In Romans 12:2 Paul says, "Do not be conformed to this world, but be transformed by the renewing of your mind (see also Ephesians 4:23).

Paul is talking about a renovation, a complete change for the better. The word *"renew"* actually means to make new from above. Man's thoughts, imaginations, and reasoning are changed through the **working of the Holy Spirit.** Dr. Bernard Ramm said, "The Spirit established the direct connection from the mind of God to the mind of the Christian."

Powerful as the Holy Spirit is He cannot do the job alone. He requires your cooperation. How, then, can you cooperate with Him?

Begin by being aware of the scriptural teaching that the Holy Spirit will empower you. Then act on that awareness by saying, "I do not have to be controlled any more by my own thoughts; I have power made available to me. I'm going to let the Holy Spirit assist me in controlling my mind. No longer can I say, 'I cannot control my thoughts,' because the Scriptures say I can."

Knowing the Scripture promise gives you hope. Part of the process of the working of the Holy Spirit is to give us the hope we need to overcome the problem.

But too many Christians think that relying upon the Holy Spirit means sitting back and saying, "Well, I'll just let him do it, I don't need to put forth any effort." Scripture doesn't say that; it teaches that we have a very definite responsibility in the process of controlling our thoughts. *I Peter 1:13* says to "gird up your minds" *(RSV)*. Gird actually means *"mental exertion."* As a Christian, you are to put out of your thoughts anything that will hinder your Christian development, your relationship with other believers, or your relationship with the Lord. When a thought comes into your mind, you have to evaluate it. You may have to say, "Wait a minute. I shouldn't dwell on that because that's going to lead me into temptation. It's going to hurt me. That's the kind of thought that really isn't going to glorify the Lord." And right then you have to get rid of that thought.

Don't leave your mind vacant, though, when you put out the negative thoughts. Jesus told the story of a man who had a demon in his house. He cast out the demon and swept the house clean and left it empty. But in the end several more demons came back and made it worse than before *(Matthew 23:43-45)*.

If you put worrisome thoughts out of your mind but do not replace them with something positive, you will probably revert back to your negative pattern of thinking. Your mind cannot be blank. If you don't fill it with something positive, it will go back to the negative because it knows that the best. It takes work and effort on your part to control the worrisome and negative thoughts. In a sense they have become your friends. They have been with you for so long that it seems unnatural to be without them. But it's time to make some new friends!

Try this: when a negative thought comes to mind, reverse it to a positive thought. If you think a critical thought about your spouse, make yourself think about three good traits your spouse has. If you feel negative about your marriage relationship, think of three good things about it. If a problem at work is bothering you, think of three or four positive aspects of your job.

You can also fill your mind with thoughts of the Lord, leaving out your problems or circumstances altogether. Sing songs of praise to Him; think through all His attributes and praise Him for them. For example: "Lord, I praise You because You are both just and merciful; I praise You because You are a God of love; I praise You because of Your mighty power as displayed in Your creation—who else could have the power to keep all the whirling atoms together so that we can have bodies and material things? Thank You for Your sense of beauty, as shown in the flowers and the animals, the mountains and the forests. Thank You for loving me enough to send Jesus Christ to live and die and rise again!" You can get so caught up in praise to Him that you forget all about your earthly circumstances.

Scripture assures us that we can control our thoughts. Overcoming worry means living a life of faith and obedience—trusting God's promises, and following His instructions. As you do these things, you may be sure that you will improve.

"But how will I know that I'm improving?" you may ask. There are three factors to consider: duration, intensity, and frequency of worry. Duration is the amount of time you spend in any one "worry session." If you used to worry for an entire day at a time, and now you worry for just half a day, that's an improvement.

In terms of intensity, if you used to get so worried and anxious that you couldn't sleep, you bit your nails, and you threw up; but now you only bite your nails and have trouble sleeping, that's improvement.

In terms of frequency, if you used to worry thirty days a month, and now you worry only twenty-five days a month, that is improvement! Often we focus our eyes on the wrong thing. "Twenty-five days last month I worried! Good grief, I'm never going to get over it." But what about the five days that you didn't worry? That is improvement!

Rest on the promises of God. You don't need to worry about the circumstances of life, because God has promised:

"Fear not, for I am with you, be not dismayed, for I am your God; I will strengthen you, I will help you, I will uphold you with my victorious right hand" *(Isaiah 41:10, RSV)*.

"But now thus says the Lord, who created you, O Jacob, he who formed you, O Israel: 'Fear not, for I have redeemed you; I have called you by name, and you are mine'" *(Isaiah 43:1, RSV)*.

Every one of us is known to God by name. You are so valuable and so important to God that if you had been the only person on earth He still would have sent His Son to die for you. That's how important you are to Him.

"I have called you by name, you are mine. When you pass through the waters I will be with you; and through the rivers, they shall not overwhelm you; when you walk through fire you shall not be burned, and the flame shall not consume you. For I am the Lord your God" *(Isaiah 43:1-3, RSV)*.

He is with us as we go through the troubled waters, and we have His presence and His strength as we live in a world that is filled with difficulties, strains and stresses. His promise is sure: *He will not leave us nor forsake us.*

ACTIVITY: Group Sharing and Praying Time: 5 minutes.

Ask the class to meet in groups of three and share a particular concern or worry that they presently have. Perhaps each person in the group could be asked the question, "If we could pray for you this week about a worry or concern, what would you have us pray about?" Conclude this time by having prayer in these small groups. Then close by reading I Samuel 12:23, "God forbid that I should sin against the Lord in ceasing to pray for you." *(KJV)*.

Distribute the "Answer to Worry and Anxiety" book and ask each person to read it this week.

Session 6

Frustration and Anger

TIME: 60 minutes
OBJECTIVES:
1. To identify the causes of frustration.
2. To implement steps to handle frustration in a creative way.

ADVANCE PREPARATION:
1. Make copies of the reproduction masters "Frustration Response Form" and "Case Studies On Frustration."

ACTIVITY: Introductory Lecture
Time: 5 minutes

FRUSTRATION

Frustrated! No matter what you want to do, and no matter what you try, *nothing* seems to work.

Frustration is an inevitable human feeling. It is a condition of wanting something and not getting it. Frustration can occur when our goals or desires are blocked. It can also be just the opposite—when we don't want something and have it forced upon us.

Frustration can also be related to our expectations. When we do a kind act for someone, we expect to be recognized and even have the deed reciprocated. When this expectation is not fulfilled, frustration and then anger can occur. In fact, frustration and anger are closely related much of the time.

Have you ever found yourself in this situation:
—wore yourself out cleaning the house all day and no one noticed?
—worked for days on a project and the boss took it for granted and never even said thanks?
—taken the kids on a special outing and all they did was bicker and fight?
—left an hour early to avoid the rush hour traffic just to discover thousands of other motorists did the same thing?
—had a day off and wanted to sleep in but woke up bright and early and couldn't get back to sleep?

ACTIVITY: Evaluations
Time: 10-15 minutes

You probably have your own list of frustrations. (Distribute copies of the "Frustration Response Form.") Ask the class to take a few minutes right now and write down six situations which frustrate them the most. Then write three frustrations which are specifically related to your family life. After they have done this have them write down how they usually respond to these frustrations.

ACTIVITY: Lecture & Sharing
Time: 5 minutes

HANDLING FRUSTRATION

Ask for volunteers to share what they wrote concerning frustration. Now that you have considered your own frustrations, let's consider a popular myth about frustrations: *Frustration always upsets a person!* That is not true. Frustration *does not* always make a person upset, disturbed, or angry! It depends upon the individual. If we think and plan carefully before a frustrating situation occurs, our predetermined course of action can help us avoid an anger reaction. So much of our disturbance and anger can be attributed to our thought life and our expectations. *It is possible to accept frustrations without becoming upset.*

Dr. Paul Hauck, a psychotherapist, put it this way: "Millions of frustrations are far more easily tolerated than we usually think. Children not finishing their dinner is not an awful frustration, just the waste of a few cents. And if a few cents bothers you, put the plate in the refrigerator until later. A person swerving in front of you in traffic is not doing something that calls for a nuclear explosion. It isn't awful to have someone honking his horn impolitely behind you—it's only slightly annoying. Not getting your raise can hurt your pocketbook, but not you, unless you let it. And that's the point, isn't it? Frustrations are not usually earthshaking to begin with—they can be tolerated quite nicely if we make the effort. Secondly, frustrations, even if they *are* severe, don't have to lead to disturbances unless we allow them to."[1]

One way to handle frustration is to accept it as being as inevitable as death. Frustrations are part of life. So why be surprised when they occur? You can choose to look at a frustration as a catastrophy or as an opportunity for growth. It is your choice!

ACTIVITY: Bible Study
Time: 5-10 minutes

THE BIBLE AND FRUSTRATION

Ask the class to move into groups of three and search through the Scriptures to discover passages which can help a person handle frustration. Give them five minutes for this study. As you ask for responses be sure to ask each person how the verse can be applied specifically. Ask for an example or an illustration.

ACTIVITY: Lecture
Time: 10-15 minutes

The scripture provides some insight into the problem of frustration. Several passages indicate the proper response that we should have to frustration:

"Consider it wholly joyful, my brethren, whenever you are enveloped in or encounter trials of any sort, or fall into various temptations. Be assured and understand that the trial and proving of your faith bring out endurance and steadfastness and patience" *(James 1:2-3, Amplified)*.

"[You should] be exceedingly glad on this account, though now for a little while you may be distressed by trials and suffer temptations, so that [the genuineness] of your faith may be tested" *(I Peter 1:6-7, Amplified)*.

"Blessed, happy, to be envied is the man who is patient under trial and stands up under temptation, for when he has stood the test and been approved he will receive [the victor's] crown of life which God has promised to those who love Him" *(James 1:12, Amplified)*.

Many temptations are frustrations and some frustrations can become temptation to sin. But the Word of God indicates the attitude we should have in these situations.

THE SOURCE OF FRUSTRATION

Frustration occurs in many forms. You may experience frustration in the area of your wishes, desires, ambitions, hopes, hungers, instinct, or even your will. You may often respond to frustration with anger. If you are hungry and cannot eat, you may become angry. If you are frightened by something and cannot run away, you may become angry. If you want to join a certain club and cannot, you may become angry.

When you are frustrated, you must consider the source of your frustration. Objects, situations, or other people may be the cause. Your friends, father, mother, wife, husband, children, or employer could be the source of frustration. You can be frustrated just as easily by someone you dislike as by the one you love the most.

You could also be frustrated by what some call the laws of nature. If you are hungry, you could be frustrated by an empty refrigerator. If you have looked forward to playing tennis on your first day off in three weeks and it rains on that day, you will be disappointed and frustrated.

Even your values or moral system can frustrate you and deter you from fulfilling certain desires. Some Christians have been heard to say, "If only I weren't a Christian, I could do that and really enjoy it!" Even though this person wants to retain his value system, it can be very frustrating. Sometimes we tend to blame God for our frustration because we feel that He places too many limitations upon us or does not give us what we think we deserve.

FRUSTRATION AND ANGER

Ask the participants to turn to a person next to them and discuss for one minute the question, "Why does frustration lead to anger?" Ask for several responses at the end of one minute and then proceed with your lecture.

"Why does frustration lead to anger?" The basic assumptions that we have about life can cause anger to arise out of frustration. Frustration may begin with the desire for something—"I want something." Now, desires are

---

1. Paul Hauck, *Overcoming Frustration and Anger*, (Philadelphia, Pa.: Westminster Press, 1974), p. 65.

natural; we all have wants and desires. We set goals and we want them to come true. But we must distinguish between "I want something" and "I must have it." If you can distinguish between the two, you may not become so upset.

When we say "I want something" we are sometimes saying, "I *must* have it. I've got to have it or else. If I don't get it, it's going to be awful. I've got to have my way, and if anyone blocks me they are terrible. In fact, if they don't let me get my way, then that's just a sign that they don't love me." These statements only help to create anger within us. We assume that we have to have our way and are frustrated because this should not happen to us.

Perhaps we should ask the question, "Why not?" Why shouldn't we experience frustration just like everyone else? We are not immune to it. It can be a growth experience. And it will be if we add another phrase to the initial statement, "I want something." "I want something, but it is all right if I don't get it. It is not the end of the world. I can live without it and can adjust and find an alternative."

Learning to live without something can often bring a greater level of satisfaction to our lives. This is not to say that we totally give up and never forge ahead. It is just that we do not allow ourselves to become upset by the various frustrations of life. If we do, the result is an emotional response which most people call anger.

ACTIVITY: Evaluation
Time: 15 minutes

Here are some statements that people have made indicating their wants or desires. (Distribute copies of the "Case Studies in Frustration.")

For example, "I want my husband to notice the clean house that I've spent seven hours slaving over today." If the husband does not notice the clean house, the wife may either give him the cold shoulder or a vesuvian eruption over his lack of sensitivity, consideration, and appreciation.

The following statement might help the wife to accept her husband's lack of appreciation: "I want my husband to notice the clean house that I've spent seven hours slaving over today. But if he doesn't, that is all right too. My happiness and sense of satisfaction do not depend upon his response. I did not clean it up solely for his response but because it needed to be cleaned. I feel better about the house and my effort. His appreciation would be an added benefit."

Divide the class into groups of four and assign each group two of the statements found in the reproduction master, "Case Studies in Frustration." Ask them to work together to develop responses to their two statements. Ask for several responses. Write a response to each of these studies which would help the person involved accept the frustration.

Now consider another step that can lessen the amount of frustration that you experience. When you want something, do you let others know about it or is it an unspoken expectation? Other people are not mind readers and they will not know what you want unless you share it with them. Telling the children or your spouse what you expect assists them in meeting your needs. Often they are grateful because you brought your desires out into the open. And if they do not respond as you expected, you do not have to become angry. You can learn to adjust and adapt. You can also learn to communicate your needs to them in a clearer and more positive manner. This will increase the likelihood of your desires being fulfilled. If one approach does not work, try another.

Conclude the session with prayer.

Session 7

What is Anger?

TIME: 45-50 minutes
OBJECTIVES:

1. To identify and clarify the meaning of the word anger.

2. To identify biblical terms for anger.
3. To assist participants in identifying the type of anger they experience.

ADVANCE PREPARATION:
1. Have paper, pencils and several boxes of crayons available.
2. Have available the overhead projector and transparency, "Three Words for Anger in the Greek New Testament."

ACTIVITY: Lecture and Agree/Disagree Statements
Time: 10-15 minutes

Begin this session by asking members to write their own definitions of anger. (Provide paper and pencils). Ask for several to give their definitions; do not share your definition yet.

Since frustrations may cause anger, we ought to consider exactly what we mean by anger. The American Heritage Dictionary describes anger as a strong, usually temporary displeasure but does not specify the manner of expressions. You can be just as angry while keeping silent as you can while yelling at someone.

The words *rage* and *fury* are used to describe intense, uncontained, explosive emotion. Fury is thought of as being destructive but rage can be considered justified by certain circumstances.

Another word for anger is *wrath*—fervid anger that seeks vengeance or punishment. *Resentment* is usually used to signify suppressed anger brought about by a sense of grievance. *Indignation* is a feeling which results when you see the mistreatment of someone or something which is very important to you.

A simple definition of anger is a strong feeling of irritation or displeasure.

Prior to this session write these two agree/disagree statements on a transparency or the chalkboard. Ask the group to indicate their response by raising their hands as to whether they agree or disagree or ask those who agree to stand up and then ask those who disagree to stand up after the others have sat down. After you have done this for both statements ask for several to share why they answered the statement as they did.

Agree	Disagree	
_____	_____	It is a sign of spiritual and emotional immaturity for a person to be angry at another individual.
_____	_____	The Bible teaches that we should avoid people who get angry much of the time.

ACTIVITY: Lecture and Evaluation
Time: 10-15 minutes

The Word of God has much to say about anger and uses a number of words to describe the various types of anger. In the Old Testament, the word for anger actually meant "nostril" or "nose." In ancient Hebrew psychology, the nose was thought to be the seat of anger. The phrase "slow to anger" literally means "long of nose." Synonyms used in the Old Testament for anger include ill-humor and rage *(Esther 1:12)*, overflowing rage and fury *(Amos 1:11)*, and indignation *(Jeremiah 15:17)*. The emotion of anger can be the subject of the scripture even though the exact word is not present. Anger can be implied through words such as revenge, cursing, jealousy, snorting, trembling, shouting, raving, and grinding the teeth.

Several words are used for anger in the New Testament. It is important to note the distinction between these words. Many people have concluded that the scripture contradicts itself because in one verse we are taught not to be angry and in another we are admonished to "be angry and sin not." Which is correct and which should we follow?

One of the words used most often for anger in the New Testament is *Thumas*. (Use the overhead transparency). It describes anger as a turbulent commotion or a boiling agitation of feelings. This type of anger blazes up into a sudden explosion. It is an outburst from inner indignation and is similar to a match which quickly ignites into a blaze but then burns out rapidly. This type of anger is mentioned twenty times in passages such as Ephesians 4:31 and Galatians 5:20. We are to control this type of anger.

Another type of anger mentioned only

three times in the New Testament, and never in a positive sense, is *Parorgismos*. This is anger that has been provoked. It is characterized by irritation, exasperation, or embitterment.

". . . do not ever let your wrath—your exasperation, your fury or indignation—last until the sun goes down" *(Ephesians 4:26, Amplified)*.

"Again I ask, Did Israel not understand?—Did the Jews have no warning that the Gospel was to go forth to the Gentiles, to all the earth? First, there is Moses who says, I will make you jealous of those who are not a nation; with a foolish nation I will make you angry" *(Romans 10:19, Amplified)*.

The most common New Testament word for anger is *Orgé*. It is used forty-five times and means a more settled and long lasting attitude which is slower in its onset but more enduring. It often includes revenge. This kind of anger is similar to coals on a barbecue slowly warming up to red and then white hot and holding this temperature until the cooking is done.

There are two exceptions where this word is used and revenge is not included in its meaning. In Ephesians 4:26 we are taught not to "let the sun go down on your anger." Mark 3:5 records Jesus as having looked upon the Pharisees "with anger." In these two verses the word means an abiding and sealed habit of the mind which is aroused under certain conditions against evil and injustice. This is the type of anger that Christians are encouraged to have—the anger that includes no revenge.

The basic overall theme of scripture concerning anger is that it will be a part of life. It is not to be denied, but is to be controlled. Certain types of anger are not healthy and should be put away. Anger should be aroused against definite injustices and then used properly.

What about the type of anger that you experience? What is it like? How would you classify it as you read these definitions? Take a few moments right now and try to think of some examples of each of these types of anger in your own life. Write down the situation and circumstances and describe the results of this anger. Describe how you felt at the time and the reaction of others to you. (Give the participants time to complete this and then ask for several responses).

ACTIVITY: Identifying Inner Feelings Through Expression
Time: 15 minutes

Provide every person with a blank piece of paper and with several crayons of various colors. Ask them to draw a symbolic picture of how they feel when they become angry. When everyone has completed this, ask for some volunteers to exhibit their drawings to the class, but do not have them explain the drawings. Ask for some opinions and observations from others as to the meaning of the drawings. Then have those who drew them explain what they represent.

Conclude the session with prayer.

Session 8 and 9
The Causes and Handling of Anger

TIME: 2 hours
OBJECTIVES:
1. To identify the causes of anger.
2. To clarify and apply biblical teaching concerning anger.
3. To develop specific steps to handle anger in a healthy manner.

ADVANCE PREPARATION:
1. Have available the overhead projector and transparencies, "Anger," "Anger and the Body," and "The Bible and Anger."
2. Make copies of the reproduction master, "Scripture Application Form."
3. Have available a copy of the book, "*An*

Answer to Anger and Frustration," for each class member. Distribute these at the conclusion of Session 9 and ask them to read the book to reinforce all that you have taught.

Note: These two sessions have been combined so that you can conclude a session at your choice of a stopping point. If there is an overabundance of discussion and questions you may need to extend this topic for an additional session. It is very important to give sufficient time to this important topic. (Be sure to use the transparencies for this presentation.)

ACTIVITY: Lecture
Time: 2 hours

What are the causes of anger? (Use the transparency, "Anger.")

Unfortunately the vast majority of people never realize that anger like depression is simply a form of message that we are sending to ourselves. Anger is the result of something else occurring within our life and when we can learn to go beyond anger and discover the cause we have then started on the process of solving our anger difficulties. Anger has these basic causes: *hurt, frustration,* and *fear.* Sometimes *injustice* is given as a cause but this may encompass these three.

When a person experiences *hurt* such as rejection, criticism, physical or emotional pain a very normal reaction is anger. We strike back and counterattack that which we feel is causing the pain.

Remember when Jesus looked at the Pharisees with anger? The passage stated that he was "grieved at their hardness of heart" *(Mark 3:5).* He was hurt at that time.

Another cause of anger is *frustration.* This we have discussed at some length in a previous session.

Fear also causes anger. When we are afraid of something, we often do not act afraid, instead we become angry. For some reason anger is more comfortable than fear. Perhaps it is because we are on the offensive rather than the defensive. **WHEN YOU ARE AFRAID AND ACT IN ANGER YOU CONFUSE OTHERS AROUND YOU.** You are not telling them what you are really feeling inside and all they can do is respond to your anger. Unfortunately, in most cases anger, begats anger.

Take the example of the husband who is home every night from work at 6:00. One night he is late. 6:40, 7:00, 7:30 goes by and not a word from him. All this time his wife is becoming increasingly more worried, concerned, and fearful. She begins thinking that something awful has happened to him. Finally about 8:00 he comes in and announces that he is home and asks if there is any dinner left. Instead of going to him and sharing her fear and concern she responds with "Well, where have you been? You sure are inconsiderate not letting me know that you were going to be late, etc." You can probably think of other situations similar to this.

When you are angry, ask yourself these questions. Do I feel hurt? Am I experiencing frustration over something? What am I frustrated about? Am I afraid of something at this time? Write these on a 3 x 5 card and carry it with you to remind you.

If you are with another person who is angry, instead of becoming angry at their anger, perhaps with sensitivity and compassion you could ask them, "Are you feeling hurt over something right now? Are you frustrated about a situation at this time? Or, are you in some way afraid?"

THE RESULTS OF ANGER

What are the results of anger? Are they constructive or destructive? If they are destructive, do they have to be? How does anger affect one's body? How does it affect family life?

Anger motivates a person to hate, wound, damage, annihilate, despise, scorn, disdain, loathe, vilify, curse, despoil, ruin, demolish, abhor, abominate, desolate, ridicule, tease, kid, get even with, laugh at, humiliate, goad, shame, criticize, scold, bawl out, irritate, beat up, fight, compete with, crush, offend, or bully another person. All of these are definitely negative!

The first time we see the effects of anger in the scripture, they are very destructive. "But for Cain and his offering He had no respect or regard. So Cain was exceedingly angry and indignant, and he looked sad and depressed. And the Lord said to Cain, 'Why are you angry?' " *(Genesis 4:5-6, Amplified)*.

Cain was angry at his brother. Why? Because Abel's sacrifice was acceptable and his was not. Inwardly Cain experienced anger; the result was murder *(4:8)*. Cain was alienated from his brother, from others, and from God. His anger led to murder and to extreme loneliness.

In another instance in the scripture we find an example of a father who, because of his displaced anger, almost killed his son. Saul was angry, envious and jealous of David. The scripture describes the scene: "Then Saul's anger was kindled against Jonathan, and he said to him, 'You son of a perverse, rebellious woman, do not I know that you have chosen the son of Jesse to your own shame, and to the shame of your mother who bore you?' But Saul cast his spear at him to smite him, by which Jonathan knew that his father had determined to kill David" *(I Samuel 20:30, 33, Amplified)*.

One of the results of anger is violence toward family members. It occurred in the scripture and it occurs everyday. Today, police receive more calls for family conflicts than they do for aggravated assault, murder, and all other serious crimes put together. Over 60 percent of the homicides committed in our nation are against family members. Even the police departments are concerned about responding to calls for family conflicts because 26 percent of police fatalities occur while handling family disturbance calls!

Paul Hauck said that "reacting with anger is like throwing a cactus at someone with your bare hands; he may get hurt, but so will you!"

HANDLING ANGER

One of the best reasons for not getting angry is that anger actually prevents a person from solving problems. It is not a solution to frustration but a reaction to frustration. If your spouse is after you to work on your marriage relationship or spend more time with the children, the solution is to talk about it. Find out how your spouse really feels, and do as much as you can to enhance your relationship.

If you don't like your working conditions, what could you do? You could either attempt to improve the working atmosphere, learn to live with an undesirable, but not intolerable situation, or look for another job. Getting angry in either setting will not bring about positive, lasting improvements in which all parties are satisfied.

One way of dealing with anger is to approach it from the perspective of frustration. If anger has been brought about by frustration, it will have a tendency to disappear if the frustration is removed. If a child is having a fit because he can't have a candy bar, he will tend to control himself if the parent succumbs to his antics and gives him the candy. If a man is angry because a planned fishing trip may be suddenly cancelled, he will tend to quiet down if he is able to go on that trip. If you are angry because a child is not responding to your attempts at discipline, your anger will subside when he begins behaving.

The point to remember is that the energy of anger does not have to be unleashed in a manner that will hurt or destroy. Instead it can be used in a constructive manner to *eliminate* the frustration. If the original frustration cannot be eliminated, many individuals learn to accept substitute goals and thereby find nearly as much and sometimes even greater satisfaction.

Remember the three questions that we suggested you ask yourself. (Ask class members to restate these questions for you.)

Becoming hateful and desiring revenge is only a short step beyond being angry. Anger is usually accompanied by thoughts of how to get even with the other person instead of how to love that person and help him respond in a way that would be positive. How can we make a friend out of someone who is angry at us?

Reacting with anger is like pouring gasoline on a fire that is already blazing. A chemical retardant would be far better! Proverbs 15:1 illustrates an appropriate response. "A soft answer turneth away wrath; but grievous words stir up anger" *(KJV)*.

(Ask the participants to turn to the person sitting next to them and for one minute discuss, "How can a person actually apply and follow Proverbs 15:1." Then ask for several responses.)

This verse does not say that the other's anger will be turned away *immediately,* but in time it will happen. Remember that you will have to plan your verbal and nonverbal response to this person well in advance and even practice it if you expect it to happen. If you wait until you are in the heat of the altercation, you will not (and cannot because of physical changes) be able to change your old angry way of reacting. Visualizing and practising the scriptural teaching in advance prepares you to make the proper response.

Why do you become angry at your family members when they don't respond to you? Why do you get angry at the kids when they don't pick up their room, mow the lawn, or dry the dishes properly? Anger expressed by yelling at a son who does not mow the lawn carefully does not teach him how to do it correctly. Angry words directed to a sloppy daughter do not teach her how to be neat! Step-by-step instruction (even if it has been given before) can help solve the problem.

Another result of anger is that you become a carrier of a very infectious germ—anger itself! If you respond in anger, others around you can easily catch the germ. If you become angry at your spouse, don't be surprised if he or she responds in like manner! You gave your husband or wife an example to follow. Your spouse is responsible for his or her own emotional responses but you still modeled the response. Perhaps if you respond with a kind but firm response, your spouse could follow this example.

Proverbs 22:24-25 illustrates this principle: "Make no friendships with a man given to anger, and with a wrathful man do not associate, lest you learn his ways and get yourself into a snare" *(Amplified).* This man is one who's life is consumed by anger. He just continually rages hostility and anger. He is a hothead of the highest degree. "A man of wrath stirs up strife, and a man given to anger commits and causes much transgression" *(Proverbs 29:22, Amplified).*

ANGER AND YOUR BODY

Have you ever considered what happens to your body when you experience strong anger? (Use the overhead transparency, "Anger and The Body.") Many physical changes occur. Sugar pours into the system, creating energy. Your blood pressure increases, your heart beats faster, and blood containing needed nourishment circulates more rapidly through your body. Your blood clots much more quickly than normal. Additional adrenalin is released. The pupils of your eyes dilate which mobilizes you for action. Your muscles tense up—in fact, the muscles at the outlet of the stomach can squeeze down so tightly that it is difficult for anything to leave your stomach while you are angry. The digestive tract can become so spastic that severe pains are felt during or after the time you are angry.

Your blood pressure may increase from 130 to 230. Your heart beats faster—often up to 220 or higher. People have had strokes during a fit of anger because of the increased blood pressure. During anger, the arteries of the heart can squeeze down hard enough to produce angina pectoris or even a fatal coronary attack.

Dr. Leo Madow stated, "Hemorrhage of the brain is usually caused by a combination of hypertension and cerebral arteriosclerosis. It is sometimes called apoplexy or stroke and may have a strong emotional component, as is shown by such expressions as 'Apoplectic with rage' and 'Don't get so mad, you'll burst a blood vessel!' Anger can produce the hypertension which explodes the diseased cerebral artery, and a stroke results. Not only does repressed anger produce physical symptoms from headaches to hemorrhoids, but it can also seriously aggravate already existing physical illnesses. Even if the illness is organic, anger can play an important role in how we respond to it. If we get angry at having a physical sickness and being disabled, unable to work, with added financial burdens, the anger can prolong both illness and convalescence."[1]

---

1. Leo Madow, *Anger—How to Recognize and Cope With It,* (Totowa, N.J.: Charles Scribner's Sons, 1972), p. 85.

What happens when this anger is not released? Your body remains prepared for action. Your heart is still beating rapidly, blood pressure is still up, and blood chemical changes are taking place.

JESUS AND ANGER

Jesus Christ experienced anger in His life, and for good reason. Norman V. Hope in *How to Be Good and Mad* gives some examples of Christ's anger.

"The gospel records make it perfectly plain that He could, on occasion, feel blazing anger and, feeling it, could and did give emphatic expression to it. For example, in Mark, chapter 3, the story is told of His healing a man with a withered hand on the Sabbath. When some protested that it was altogether improper to heal a man on the Sabbath, Jesus was indignant at their stubbornly perverted sense of values. The Scripture says that He 'looked round about on them with anger, being grieved for the hardness of their hearts.' In Matthew 23, the account is given of Jesus' blasting the scribes and Pharisees, whom He describes as 'hypocrites' for the revolting contrast between their high religious profession and their low, irreligious practices. And in John 2 it is recorded that Jesus cleansed the Temple of its money changers, insisting that His Father's house must not be made a house of merchandise."[2]

Jesus expressed indignation which means irritation or annoyance *(Luke 18:15)*. This emotion is also expressed in *Matthew 20:24; 21:15; 24:8, Mark 10:41; 14:4, Luke 13:14; II Corinthians 7:11.*

Elizabeth Skoglund said, "Christ himself was slow to anger with the woman caught in adultery because he knew her heart, and he reacted quickly against her accusers because he also knew their inner thoughts. He showed anger at the disciples when they tried to keep the children from him, and yet he was tender when the multitudes pressed against him. In violent anger he chased the money changers out of the temple, but he showed only a weary disappointment when the disciples slept while he prayed in the Garden of Gethsemane.

"The most significant example of slowness to anger in the history of mankind was exhibited two thousand years ago by Jesus. Christ, the God-man crucified by the caprice of a mob and the weakness of those in authority, prayed with agonized genuineness, 'Father, forgive these people, for they don't know what they are doing' *(Luke 23:34, TLB)*. His profound comprehension of the significance of what he was doing contrasted with the total ignorance of the crowds. His sensitivity of them and their plight helped make him slow to anger indeed."[3]

Jesus experienced anger and felt free to let it show. He clearly and constructively expressed His anger.

CONSTRUCTIVE ANGER

It should be obvious from these examples that anger is not necessarily bad. The results of anger can be either positive or negative, constructive or damaging.

Anger is like gunpowder which, depending upon how it is directed, can blast away at injustices or can kill or maim the innocent.

When used constructively, anger can sometimes be an asset to a person. One who is angry enough may be able to accomplish great feats of strength which he would not otherwise be able to handle, such as raising a car off a loved one who is trapped underneath.

Dr. Leo Madow explains further: "Constructively used, anger can give strength both physically and mentally. Such normal outlets for anger are dependent on several factors. First, the individual must not be overwhelmed by his anger, because he is then rendered ineffective. Second, there should not be so much fear of anger that it cannot be released directly, as it will then come out in unhealthy ways. Third, opportunities for some socially acceptable outlet must exist."[4]

"Anger relates to self-esteem. The person

---

2. Norman V. Hope, "How to Be Good and Mad," *Christianity Today* (July 19, 1968).

3. Elizabeth Skoglund, *To Anger With Love*, (New York, N.Y.: Harper & Row, 1977), p. 32.
4. As quoted in H. Norman Wright, *The Christian Use of Emotional Power*, (Old Tappan, N.J.: Fleming H. Revell, 1974), pp. 111-12.

who uses anger positively likes himself better; the person who hurts himself or others with his rage likes himself less. Depending on our level of self-esteem, we will be more or less prone to angry feelings. A person with a low self-image will be more sensitive to criticism, more touchy, more easily made angry. Within ourselves we change almost daily depending on how life is proceeding. When my life is smooth, I feel better about myself and am less likely to be easily provoked. But if everything on a given day has gone wrong, I may become irritable with little or no provocation. Only God really knows where we are inside, and his condemnation and reward for how we handle anger is bound up in how strong the temptation was for us at a given time. People judge us by our outward appearance. God judges us by our inward climate—what we feel about ourselves, how vulnerable we are to a given stimulus, how hard we try to react in a right way."5

Ephesians 4:26 tells us to "be angry and sin not." (Ask the class participants to spend three minutes discussing with the person next to them, "How can a person be angry and sin not?" Ask for several examples.)

Earlier we saw that this is one of the passages where anger is legitimate. The word *angry* in this verse means an anger which is an abiding and settled habit of the mind, and which is aroused under certain conditions. You are aware of this kind of anger and it is under control. There is a legitimate reason for this anger. Your reasoning powers are involved and when reason is present, anger such as this is proper. The scriptures not only permit it but on some occasions **demand it!** Perhaps this sounds strange to some who have thought for years that anger is all wrong. But the Word of God does state that *we are to be angry!*

Paul actually commended the Corinthians in one place for their aroused indignation against the believer who had married his own mother. *(See I Corinthians 5:1-2, II Corinthians 7:11).* This is righteous anger. It is not sinful when it is properly directed. Such anger must be an abiding, settled attitude of righteous indignation against sin, coupled with appropriate action.

There are **three main characteristics** of righteous anger. Ask the class for their opinion on what these characteristics are. First of all it must be **controlled**. It is not a heated, unrestrained passion. Even if the cause is legitimate and is directed at an injustice, uncontrolled anger can cause an error in judgment and increase the difficulty. The mind must be in control of the emotions so that the ability to reason is not lost. "Be angry and sin not." Perhaps the way this is accomplished is related to the scriptural teaching in *Proverbs 14:29* and *16:32,* "Be slow to anger." This kind of anger is not a direct result of immediate frustration.

(Divide the class into groups of three. Ask them to take five minutes to discuss how a person can be "slow to anger." What steps could be taken to put this passage into practice? Ask for several responses.)

Second, **there must be no hatred, malice, or resentment.** Anger that harbors a counter-attack only complicates the situation. Perhaps our best example of how to respond is Jesus' reaction to the injustices delivered against Him.

"When he was reviled and insulted, He did not revile or offer insult in return; [when] He was abused and suffered, He made no threats [of vengeance]; but He trusted [Himself and everything] to Him who judges fairly" *(I Peter 2:23 Amplified).*

"Beloved, never avenge yourselves, but leave the way open for [God's] wrath; for it is written, Vengeance is Mine, I will repay [requite], says the Lord" *(Romans 12:19, Amplified).*

The final characteristic of righteous anger is that its motivation is unselfish. When the motivation is selfish, pride and resentment are usually involved. Anger should be directed not at the wrong done to oneself but at the injustice done to others.

It is possible to confront another person

---

6. Elizabeth Skoglund, *To Anger With Love* (New York, N.Y.: Harper & Row, 1977), p. 103.

without being angry. We need not confuse anger with confrontation and firmness. Anger usually springs from a desire to defend ourselves or to get someone to do what we want. You can share your feelings of frustration over the very same things, but in a nonviolent, nonattacking manner.

THE CHOICE IS YOURS

Once a person discovers he is angry, how can he deal with that anger? What choices are available to him? There are four basic ways to deal with anger. (Use the overhead transparency, "Anger.")

One way is to *repress* it. Don't even admit that you are angry. Ignore its presence. "This repression is often unconscious, but it is **not healthy!** Repressing anger is like placing a wastebasket full of paper in a closet and setting fire to it. The fire will either burn itself out *or* it could set the entire house on fire and burn it down. The energy produced by anger cannot be destroyed. It must be converted or directed into another channel.

"One outlet for repressed anger is accidents. Perhaps you have met people who are **accident-prone.** Unfortunately, their accidents may involve other people as well as themselves. A man who is angry may slam a door on his own hand or someone else's. He may wash windows for his wife when he would rather be watching a game on TV and put his hand through the window. His driving manifests his anger when he 'accidentally' runs over the rose bushes.

"Repressed anger can easily take its toll on your body by giving you a vicious headache. Your gastrointestinal system—that thirty-foot tube extending from the mouth to the rectum—reacts beautifully to repressed anger. You may experience difficulty in swallowing, nausea and vomiting, gastric ulcer, constipation, or diarrhea. The most common cause of ulcerative colitis is repressed anger. Repressed anger can affect the skin through pruritus, itching, and neurodermatitis. Respiratory disorders such as asthma are common effects and the role of anger in coronary thrombosis is fairly well accepted."[6]

Anger and depression are among the most common problems of those who seek professional counseling. Furthermore, they are not new problems. Throughout biblical history great men of God labored under these two emotions. Jonah is perhaps the classic example. He was sent by God to warn the people of Nineveh about their sinfulness. He completed this task successfully to the point where the king of Nineveh turned from his sin and commanded his people to do likewise. In turn God "abandoned his plan to destroy them, and didn't carry it through" *(Jonah 3:10, TLB).*

The biblical record goes on to say: "This change of plans made Jonah very angry. He complained to the Lord about it: 'This is exactly what I thought you'd do, Lord when I was there in my own country and you first told me to come here . . . For I knew you were a gracious god, merciful, slow to get angry, and full of kindness; I knew how easily you could cancel your plans for destroying these people. Please kill me, Lord; I'd rather be dead than alive . . .' Then the Lord said, 'Is it right to be *angry* about *this*?' " So Jonah went out and sat sulking on the east side of the city *(Jonah 4:1-5, TLB).*

However, all does not go well with Jonah; depressed, he sits under a vine. The vine dries, and the heat from the sun becomes intense. Then in a last recorded dialogue with God, Jonah states, "It is right for me to be angry enough to die" *(Jonah 4:9, TLB).* Anger turned outward made Jonah desire Nineveh's destruction. Then he sought the cooling comfort of the vine, and his anger turned inward and became depression. At one point Jonah was content just to sit and "hole up," and at another point he wished for, indeed asked for, death.

While depression and anger are not usually linked this clearly in Scripture, they are presented as acceptable emotions when handled responsibly.[7]

---

6. Wright, pp. 121-22.
7. Elizabeth Skoglund, *To Anger With Love,* (New York, N.Y.: Harper & Row, 1977). pp. 78-79.

Anger and hatred can lead to further complications. But so does repression. Repressed anger or anger held in or turned inward often turns into depression. In our unconscious attempt to handle the emotion, we bring harm to our own body.

As David Augsburger writes, "Repressed anger hurts and keeps on hurting. If you always deal with it simply by holding it firmly in check or sweeping it under the rug, without any form of release or healing, it can produce rigidity and coldness in personality."[8]

Many large manufacturing companies dispose of their industrial waste material by pumping it into underground mines or abandoned wells. This works for a while but eventually it will pollute other water systems or burst out into the open through another channel. Our repressed anger is our own unrefined waste material.

Dr. William Menninger said, "Do not talk when angry but after you have calmed down. Sometimes we push each other away and the problem between us festers and festers. Just as in surgery, free and adequate drainage is essential if healing is to take place.[9]

Anger is an emotion that must be recognized and accepted. "When you repress or suppress those things which you don't want to live with," suggests John Powell in *Why Am I Afraid To Love*? "you don't really solve the problem because you don't bury the problem dead—you bury it alive." God created us with the capacity for emotional reactions. We need to recognize and accept our anger for what it is. Only then can we learn to use it wisely and properly.

A similar way to handle anger is to *suppress* it. A person choosing this means is aware of his anger but chooses to hold it in and not let people know he is angry. In some situations this may be healthy and wise, but eventually the anger needs to be recognized and drained away in a healthy manner. But the person who *always* stuffs anger away is a sad case. The constant effort of holding back and keeping it in results in an incredible waste of energy.

Though their cheerful smiling exteriors make it seem otherwise, *Stuffers* are usually very unhappy people. Some stuffers literally stuff themselves eating enormous amounts of food, partly a way of punishing themselves for the sin of anger.

Often a person chooses to suppress his anger when the person with whom he is angry could react with more force or authority. For example, an employer calls in one of his employees and angrily confronts him about some alleged problem. The employee feels his own anger rising but realizes that if he expresses his anger to his boss he could lose his job. So he suppresses his anger—until he arrives home. His wife greets him when he walks in the door and he replies with an angry snarl. This surprises her and she will either react by snapping back at him or by following her husband's previous example and suppressing her anger. But then her teenage son walks in and she vents her pent-up anger upon the unsuspecting boy. He takes out his anger on the younger brother who in turn kicks the dog who bites the cat who scratches the three-year-old who takes out her frustration by pulling off the head of her Barbie doll! This simple process of directing your anger on a less threatening person is called displacement. It may help you for a moment but it can set up a long-lasting chain of events that infects the lives of others like an epidemic.

Guilt is another reason for displacing anger. If you are furious with your mother but believe that it is wrong to get angry with one's mother, you may find yourself exploding at other older women. Or you may use displacement to avoid humiliating yourself. You are traveling with your husband and trying to make mileage on a particular day. You take a wrong turn and go fifty miles in the wrong direction. You then project the blame onto your husband and accuse him of misguiding you.

Is the cause for your anger realistic? Is it reasonable? Is it born out of frustration? Does it come from unexpressed desires? Deal with the problem directly. If you have a disagreement with your employer over office procedures, the solution is not to go home and complain to your wife or to another employee.

---

8. David Augsburger, *Be All You Can Be*, (Carol Stream, Ill.: Creation House), p. 60.
9. William Menninger, "Behind Many Flaws of Society," *National Observer*, (August 31, 1964), p. 18.

Talk with him and attempt to resolve the problem. If this is not practical, then you must put up with the situation and find other constructive outlets for your anger when it arises. The ideal solution is to practice various responses to the cause of your frustration.

If the cause for you anger is not legitimate, the problem is within you. If you get angry with your wife because she does not cook meals the way your mother did, then you had better begin by recognizing that your wife is not your mother! Allow her to develop her own cooking skills and try some new recipes. Then learn to compromise on some of your expectations.

Dr. James Dobson was once asked, "Many psychologists seem to feel that all anger should be ventilated or verbalized. They say it is emotionally and physically harmful to repress or withold any intense feeling. Can you harmonize this scientific understanding with the scriptural commandment that 'every man (should) be swift to hear, slow to speak, slow to wrath' *(James 1:19, KJV)*?" His response was very helpful: "We must harmonize the psychological finding that anger should be ventilated with the biblical commandment that we be 'slow to wrath.' Personally, I do not find these objectives to be in contradiction. God does not want us to repress our anger—sending it unresolved into the memory bank. Why else did the apostle Paul tell us to settle our irritations before sundown each day, effectively preventing an accumulation of seething hostility with the passage of time?

"But how can intense negative feelings be resolved or ventilated without blasting away at the offender—an act which is specifically prohibited by the scripture? Are there other ways of releasing pent-up emotions? Yes, including those that follow:

"By making the irritation a matter of prayer.

"By explaining our negative feelings to a mature and understanding 'third party' who can advise and lead.

"By going to an offender and showing a spirit of love and forgiveness.

"By understanding that God often permits the most frustrating and agitating events to occur, so as to teach us patience and help us grow.

"By realizing that no offense by another person could possibly equal our guilt before God, yet He has forgiven us; are we not obligated to show the same mercy to others?"[10]

It is interesting that some psychologists today advocate cutting loose with all of your anger regardless of how you do it or the results. But other psychological research in the past few years indicates negative results of ventilating all of one's anger. The findings show that as the level of verbal aggression increases (anger poured out) the level of physical aggression increases dramatically. Discussing things calmly, getting information bearing on the issue, and calling for help from outsiders helps to settle the problems and keep the possibility for physical violence lower.[11]

Suppressing anger does have some merit, however, especially if it helps you relax, cool down, and begin to act in a rational manner. The Word of God has something to say about this type of suppression.

Ask the class members to look up these passages and summarize each one with 2-4 words. Ask them to do this individually. Then ask for several responses.

"He who is slow to anger has great understanding, but he who is hasty of spirit exposes and exalts his folly" *(Proverb 14:29, Amplified.)* This man is one who actually suppresses strife in the beginning so it doesn't break out.

"He who is slow to anger is better than the mighty, and he who rules his own spirit than he who takes a city" *(Proverbs 16:32, Amplified)*.

"Good sense makes a man restrain his anger, and it is his glory to overlook a transgression or an offense" *(Proverb 19:11, Amplified)*.

"Make no friendships with a man given to anger, and with a wrathful man do not associate" *(Proverb 22:24, Amplified)*.

---

10. James Dobson, *Dr. James Dobson Talks About Anger* (Glendale, Calif.: G/L Publications, Regal Books Division, 1975), pp. 16-17.
11. Murray Straus, "Leveling, Civility and Violence in the Family," *Journal of Marriage and Family* (February 1974), pp. 13, 21.

"A (self-confident) fool utters all his anger, but a wise man keeps it back and stills it" (*Proverb 29:11, Amplified*). This passage means that the person does not give unbridled license to his anger but sort of hushes it up and puts it in the background. It also means anger is overcome.

"I [Nehemiah] was very angry when I heard their cry and these words. I thought it over, then rebuked the nobles and officials" (*Nehemiah 5:6-7, Amplified*). One version translates this verse as "I consulted with myself."

"Understand [this], my beloved brethren. Let every man be quick to hear, [a ready listener], slow to speak, slow to take offense and to get angry" (*James 1:19, Amplified*).

The individual who practices and exerts self-control will find that his anger level actually decreases. He will not become *as* angry as if he were to simply cut loose with his first reaction. A calm consideration of the cause for the anger and the results will help you handle the situation properly. Count to ten, taking a couple of deep breaths.

Expressing your anger is a third way to handle it. Some people think you should express exactly how you feel no matter what or who is involved. They feel this is psychologically healthy and necessary in order to live a balanced life.

There are many different ways to express anger. One is to react with violent passion, yelling harsh words, swearing, all with tremendous emotion. This can bring results but you may not care for them. If you are allowed the freedom to react in this way, shouldn't the other person have the same freedom to react to you in this manner?

But you can also express your anger by riding your bike around the block, digging in the garden for an hour, or beating on a stuffed pillow. Some of these people are called *Doers*. You can write down exactly how you feel when you get angry, especially if it is difficult to verbalize your feelings. These methods may sound strange but they should not be discounted. They have been used to help many people overcome their difficulties with anger.

If both you and your spouse are angry, it is better, if you are working it off physically, to do it separately. For some reason the anger disappears faster.

What habitual *Doers* need to keep in mind, however, is that while "murdering a tennis ball, polishing a floor or sewing a fine seam may make them feel better these activities are hardly ever directly related to the source of anger."

Everyone can and probably should be a *Doer* some of the time, but if your only way of handling anger is to escape into physical activity, ask yourself the following questions from time to time: At whom am I angry and why? How can I change things and feel better.

"The final method of dealing with anger is to *confess it*. This is . . . the best method, especially if it is coupled with an intelligent and healthy use of suppression or self-control. Confess the fact that you are angry—to yourself, to God, and to the person involved. Don't say, 'You're making me angry.' The individual is not making you angry. You are responsible for your own emotional reaction toward him. You could say, 'The way our discussion is going, I'm getting angry. I'm not sure that's the best reaction so perhaps we could start over in our discussion.' Or, 'I'm sorry but I'm angry. What can I do now so we can resolve our differences?' Try admitting and confessing your anger."[12]

Confession used in this sense is not to mean that anger is sinful. It means admitting and facing our anger. Another way of saying this is to possess and process your anger. Accept its presence and your responsibility for being angry and do something about it in a constructive way.

Elizabeth Skoglund said, "Remember, Christ does not condemn anger. For the Christian the problem of feeling anger should never be spiritualized. The mother who feels anger at her son's low grades at school is not sinful nor does that anger have to be confessed as sin. The young man unjustly or even justly released from his job does not sin when he feels anger. Anger is a natural reaction to pain. What we do with that anger, however, may have profound spiritual implications."[13]

---

12. Wright, p. 127.
13. Skoglund, p. 89.

What about talking things over while you are still angry? Doesn't this help? Actually it is very difficult to talk rationally about problems when you are angry. Exercise or relaxation is important before people attempt to resolve their differences. When people are calm, results are more evident. Confession and time may be the proper steps in the right direction.

Not all anger is sinful or wrong! Just the admission of being angry can help you release the feeling and get the message across in an acceptable manner to the person involved. David Augsburger writes about the problem in *Caring Enough to Confront.*

"Explosive anger is 'the curse of interpersonal relations.' Vented anger may ventilate feelings and provide instant, though temporary, release for tortured emotions, but it does little for relationships."

"Clearly expressed anger is something different. Clear statements of anger feelings and angry demands can slice through emotional barriers or communications tangles and establish contact."[14]

But don't you have to be angry in order to get your point across to others? Some people don't seem to respond unless anger is a part of the message? Believe it or not, it is possible to share a complaint or a criticism with another person in a calm, well-thought-out manner that will bring about more change than if you respond to him in anger. Many couples find healthy problem solving to be a major area of dissatisfaction in their marriages.

The scripture says that a "soft answer turns away wrath." It also says that I am to "be slow to anger." I know it says that, but how can I do it? I have these people at work who every now and then get angry with me and start chewing me out with some complaint. I do get angry. How can I respond to them in a healthy way that would also be consistent with the teaching in the Bible?

Before some suggestions are given, remember, just because someone is upset with you, you don't have to become upset yourself, no matter how he says it or what he says.

(Use the bottom section of the overhead transparency, "Anger.")

1. If someone has a criticism to make of you, *stop* what you are doing and *look* directly at him. By giving your attention directly to him, the irritation may be lessened.

2. *Listen* to the person. Let him talk. *Proverbs 18:13* states: "He who answers a matter before he hears the facts, it is folly and shame to him" *(Amplified)*. Try to hear what the person is really saying. Try to hear what is behind his remarks. You may just be the object of all of his pent-up frustration, with nothing personal intended.

3. Accept the criticism as the other person's way of seeing things. From his *perspective,* his interpretation is correct. And he could be right, so don't write off the complaint. If he exaggerates, don't get hung up attempting to correct him at that time.

4. *Don't accuse* the person of being oversensitive or irrational. That won't help solve the problem that has been presented.

5. *Don't bring up another subject* or attempt to evade the present issue. *Don't joke* about the complaint because it could be very important to the other person.

6. *Be open to the criticism* and consider its validity before you respond. It could be right and this could be an opportunity for you to grow. You could even thank the person for bringing it to your attention, as this does help you know how the other person is feeling.

Consider the following passages in Proverbs from The Living Bible before you make your response.

"If you refuse criticism you will end in poverty and disgrace; if you accept criticism you are on the road to fame" *(13:18)*.

"Don't refuse to accept criticism; get all the help you can" *(23:12)*.

"It is a badge of honor to accept valid criticism" *(25:12)*.

"A man who refuses to admit his mistakes can never be successful. But if he confesses and forsakes them, he gets another chance" *(28:13)*.

7. After the person has finished sharing his complaint with you, ask for an opportunity to respond to what he has said. First, *restate* what you heard the other person say to you in order

---

14. David Augsburger, *Caring Enough to Confront* (Glendale, Calif.: G/L Publications, Regal Books Division, 1973), p. 49.

to show that you were listening and to make sure you understood everything. ***Then share what you feel and believe,*** and if the other person is correct, be sure to admit it. If you feel he is mistaken, you could defend yourself but how you share your feelings is very important.[15]

WHAT IS YOUR ANGER SAYING?

What is an answer for controlling and channeling your anger? What is your anger saying to you? What is its message? Could it be expressing a deeper hurt or desire? Behind angry looks could be fear and rejection. Underneath feelings of anger could be concealed expectations and subsequent frustrations. Inside angry statements could be hidden demands. Listen to your anger.

"You see, hostility has its root in reaction to love that is withheld or denied."

"The only cure, then, is in filling that void with love. God offers love. Unconditional love that will fill an open heart and heal the hurts."

"When you open your life to the love of God, you are unreservedly accepting God's love and God's loving way of living for yourself. Then the love of God goes to work penetrating the depths of your spirit with healing."

"A second step in opening your life to God is to absorb not only the assurance of His love and His loving spirit within you, but His Word. Read the Bible. Mull it over. Let it soak down deep into your mind. Memorize it. There is power in stocking your memory and your heart with what is lovely, good, wholesome, true" *(cf. Philippians 4:8).*

"The truth of God absorbed into the mind and heart can act as a disinfectant to deal with the accumulated infections of our sinfulness."

"David, the ancient king of Israel, said, 'I store Thy Word within my heart, to keep myself from sinning against Thee' *(Psalms 119:11, Moffatt).*

Distribute a copy of the answer book ***"An Answer to Anger and Frustration"*** and have them turn to page 52. Then distribute a copy of the reproduction master, "Scripture Application Form."

ACTIVITY: Application
Time: 10-30 minutes

(The time factor here may depend upon time available).

Ask the class to complete the form. Write out the practical ways in which you see yourself doing the things suggested in the verse. Write down when and how you will begin and the consequences that you expect. Be very specific.

Now take the following scriptures that pertain to your area of concern and complete this procedure using the outline suggested on the example form:

Ephesians 4:26
Proverbs 15:1, 18; 16:32, 19:11, 29:11.

Reviewing what the scriptures has to say about anger, use the overhead transparency, "The Bible and Anger," ("The Bible Says . . ." section) for your review. Then summarize the principles of dealing with anger using the section entitled, "What to Do With Anger."

Close the session by reading Philippians 4:9, which emphasizes the concept of practice. Encourage the class to take the time this week to find other scriptures that deal with anger, and follow the same procedure of writing out and then visualizing the scripture as a part of their life.

Conclude the session with prayer.

---

15. Adapted from John Lembo, *Help Yourself,* (Niles, Ill.: Argus Communications, 1974), pp. 42-43.

EMOTION

EMOTIONS AND FEELINGS

	My Answer	As I See My Spouse

1. Do I feel that it's all right to express my feelings and emotions and to talk about them? Or have I learned that feelings and emotions are dangerous?

2. Do I allow my emotions to flow inside me spontaneously without trying to push them down? Do I feel that I have to manufacture or make up emotions that I don't really feel in order to please others or because I think I should feel certain emotions?

3. Are there emotions that I overdo (perhaps anger, depression, self-pity)? Are there emotions that I refuse to experience (attraction, hurt, enthusiasm)?

4. Do I let my emotions add life and color to my conversations? Or do I control my emotions too much?

5. Do I use my emotions to control others and get them to do what I want them to do (perhaps to leave me alone)?

6. Do I express or talk about my emotions when they come up in the here and now, or do I save them for a later, safer time?

7. Do I feel that I have a right to be emotional, to assert my emotions without stepping on the rights of others? Do I ever use my emotions to step on the rights of others?

8. Am I willing to take reasonable risks in expressing my emotions? That is, do I experiment with emotions I ordinarily hide or avoid?

9. When others are expressing emotions, do I get scared? Do I try to get them to stop expressing their emotions?

10. What emotions are most difficult for me to express?

11. How do I feel about myself? Does the way I feel about myself prevent me from expressing my emotions or from even feeling emotions?

Session 2

1979 © Harvest House Publishers, 2861 McGaw, Irvine, California 92714
Permission is granted to reproduce this reproduction master for classroom use—not for resale.

FRUSTRATION RESPONSE FORM

Six situations which frustrate me the most are:	How do I usually respond?
1.	
2.	
3.	
4.	
5.	
6.	

The frustrations related to my family life are:	How do I usually respond?
1.	
2.	
3.	

CASE STUDIES IN FRUSTRATION

Write a response to each of these studies which would help the persons involved accept the frustration.

1. "I want to be sure to get to the sale at the store before everything is picked over. It is the only opportunity to save that much money."

2. "I sure hope that dinner is ready when I get home tonight and the kids keep quiet for a change. I don't need any hassle tonight."

3. "After all of the work that I've put in on that committee, I hope that I'm considered for the chairmanship this year. It means a lot to me to be able to lead that group, if given the chance."

4. "I've just got to get this work done today before our guests arrive. I don't know what I'll do if they arrive before I finish."

5. "After giving my son piano lessons for seven years and paying all that money, I certainly hope that he doesn't ask to quit. Last year at this time he really hassled me about it. I just don't need that."

SCRIPTURE APPLICATION FORM

EXAMPLE
Ephesians 4:31-32

Behavior or attitude to STOP	List the results of this behavior. Give several for each one.
Bitterness (Resentfulness, harshness)	
Anger (Fury—antagonism—outburst)	
Wrath (Indignation, violent anger, boiling up)	
Clamor (Brawling)	
Slander (Abusive speech)	
Positive Behavior or Attitude to BEGIN	What do you think would be the results of doing these three commands? List several for each.
Be Kind (Goodness of heart)	
Tenderhearted (Compassionate)	
Forgiveness (An action)	